Are You There, God? It's Me, Ellen

Gill Books
Hume Avenue
Park West
Dublin 12
www.gillbooks.ie

Gill Books is an imprint of M.H. Gill and Co.

Portions of Chapter 6 are based on articles previously published in *The Times* Ireland Edition on 9 April 2019. Portions of Chapter 10 are based on articles previously published in *The Times* Ireland Edition on 21 August 2017.

978 07171 88949

Edited by Emma Dunne
Proofread by Djinn von Noorden
Printed by CPI Group (UK) Ltd, Croydon, CRO 4YY
This book is typeset in 12.5 on 20pt, Sabon.

The paper used in this book comes from the wood pulp of managed forests. For every tree felled, at least one tree is planted, thereby renewing natural resources.

A CIP catalogue record for this book is available from the British Library.
5 4 3 2 1

Are You There, God? It's Me, Ellen

Ellen Coyne

Gill Books

Ellen Coyne is a news correspondent with the *Irish Independent*. She was previously Head of Politics with Joe.ie and a correspondent with *The Times* Ireland Edition. In both 2017 and 2018 she won the Newsbrands Ireland Journalism Award for political story of the year. A Waterford native, she lives in Dublin.

'This is not the book you would have expected Ellen Coyne to write, but it might just be the book she was born to write. While never shying away from the abhorrent aspects of the Church's past, *Are You There, God? It's Me, Ellen* is a clear-eyed, thought-provoking call to arms for radical reform within the institution itself. In this meticulously well-researched book, Coyne's passion for her subject is unmistakable, but it is her inherent compassion that underpins her entire argument. Get ready – this is going to inspire a thousand conversations across Ireland about the role of the Church in our society and our future.'
– Louise O'Neill

'This book will resonate with so many people. It's intelligent, personal and bound to speak to anyone with complicated feelings towards the Catholic Church. I flew through it on a "will she, won't she?" knife-edge, all the while questioning my own attitude to faith and spirituality. The perfect book for 2020 Ireland.'
– Emer McLysaght

'Coyne's spirit sings with sincerity. This is the book the Church doesn't know it needs for its own survival. Coyne's courage and honesty are in stark contrast with the institutional Church's track record. Why is this woman not the pope?'
– Justine McCarthy

For Peter,
for always helping me to keep the faith.

Prologue

Well, you think you know a person. More than that, you think you know yourself. But everybody is full of surprises. The truth first came out, appropriately, over bread and wine.

'I think,' I said, 'I might be Catholic.'

Two friends stared back at me, incredulous. Ash gathered on the ends of their cigarettes, suspended in the air in disbelief.

I was perched quite precariously on a bar stool. Across from me were these two very good friends. We were sitting in a pub smoking area around a barrel that doubled up as a table, on which ashtrays and empty white wine bottles were piling high. Picking over the remains of a cheeseboard, I'd had just enough wine to make me very earnest, very emotional and treacherously honest. So I told them. And how I'd said it was ridiculous, as though I was confessing to some problematic fetish or a heinous crime.

Still, though – Catholic? I would have raised my eyebrows, too. I don't think anyone who knows me had ever heard me say a single good thing about the Catholic Church.

The Church to me was dark and oppressive. The Catholic Church meant abuse, misogyny, homophobia, power hunger and piousness. I had scrambled to get away from it as soon as I was independent enough to, and since then I had regarded it with suspicion from a distance. I thought the Church was a relic from another time, one that we would have to politely avoid looking at as it died in front of us. As my generation defined itself by progressive social movements and historic referendums, a huge chasm opened up between us and the Church. We didn't like the Church, and the Church didn't seem to like us either, and that suited us all just fine. I was full sure after I walked away from the Church that I wouldn't cast it so much as a backwards glance, never mind think about going back to it.

Yet here I was, blurting out loud some of the weird and secret feelings I'd been having. That was the starting point of all of it. My first confession.

Chapter 1

The night I made that little confession was right in the throes of a time when trust in and regard for the Catholic Church was at its lowest. That little vignette of us, three young women deep into a bar tab and deeper in conversation, was playing out everywhere. Across the country, people were talking about things they'd never talked about before and saying things they'd never said before. It was all part of what we were unironically calling 'the national conversation'.

We were weeks away from the 2018 referendum on the Eighth Amendment – a national vote to decide if Ireland was going to lift its constitutional near-ban on abortion after over 30 years. I was a journalist who had been covering the campaign for weeks and months and even years before. More pertinently, though, I am also a woman.

Almost everything from the month before the vote has blurred together like a fever dream. I know a lot of people endured those weeks rather than lived them. It felt like the country was in a state of convulsion. It was quite a painful thing.

Both sides believed the result would say something important about the kind of country we were, in different ways. Questions about the right to autonomy and the right to life are profound enough on their own, but this vote went further than that. People ascribed all sorts of other meanings to it related to Ireland's history and Ireland's modernity, to faith, society, women, rights and wrongs.

The week before, I had gone to a drag brunch with a couple of friends I knew very well and some women I didn't know at all. As we sat around a long table clutching our syrupy cocktails, one of the women, a total stranger to me, told us about travelling for her abortion. It was an emotional thing to listen to, but a terrifying thing as well. We had no idea at that point if anything was going to change and if a story like hers would ever not be normal.

These disclosures could happen at any place, at any time. I was following canvassers for a newspaper I worked for, and sometimes people would answer the door and just burst out crying. In a town in Offaly, I watched a woman with tears in her eyes take a Yes badge from a campaigner and pin it to the inside of her coat, where it would not be seen.

I have never had to make the choice those women had to make, but I was silly to think that those awful weeks leading up to the vote wouldn't have an effect on me. It's unsettling to watch your rights as a woman being put to a popular vote.

At work, I wrote stories about all these women who offered to testify to the nation about what had happened to them under the Eighth Amendment. All these women and their personal tragedies were condensed into digestible, emotional headlines. It was like a national trial where women had to prove the trauma they had experienced was severe enough before the jury of us citizens would decide it had been wrong. These women weren't even asking for a Yes for themselves – they were asking for it not to happen to other people. And they had to ask! Afterwards, people talked about how we chose repeal by popular vote as a joyous or empowering thing. Though it never could have been done any other way, there was an element of putting it to a vote that felt kind of degrading to me.

It's easy to remember the version of Ireland in the square of Dublin Castle that was broadcast around the world, covered in the rose-tinted veneer of modernity and compassion. It felt like the scales had fallen from our eyes when we realised that many more people wanted change than we had been led to believe. A lot of people valued having a direct say on repeal, and many took heart in the fact that change came from 'the people'. But the campaign started from the point at which women had to try to win or earn their rights from their fellow citizens by proving that having to travel for healthcare is degrading and wrong. That felt grossly unfair to the women themselves and also to those of us who might have never made the choice to travel. From interviewing women who told their stories in the years after the campaign, I know that the pain of what they went through in having to use their personal experience to campaign for a Yes almost tainted the result for them.

The referendum on the Eighth Amendment was credited with changing Ireland. It also changed me. The way that the Catholic Church aggressively campaigned for a No vote during the campaign changed the way I looked at religion. There had been over 30 years of debate over abortion law in Ireland. It had trundled along, peaking in ferocity over travesties like the X case or the death of Savita Halappanavar. The referendum campaign meant that the whole nation had to go through all of those arguments again, but faster and with more intensity. It was a high-stakes last dance for the groups that had been fighting for or against reform so ferociously for years. And the Catholic Church came out swinging.

Bishops and priests were righteous and unequivocal: Catholics had an obligation to vote No. Anti-abortion leaflets started to appear at the back of churches next to donation boxes and literature about pilgrimages. Priests started to use sermons to campaign and canvass for support for their side. I started to read about the things they had said. Bishop Kevin Doran said that this was the 'final frontier', that it would be easier to justify killing older people and those with disabilities after abortion. Archbishop Eamon Martin said that abortion was 'always evil and can never be justified'. The Church's position was absolutist, pontifical and relied completely on obedience over freedom of conscience.

I wasn't sure why I was becoming so obsessed with what the Church was saying. I would immediately click into any article where a cleric was talking about abortion. Scrolling, fuming, I would turn the phone screen towards my boyfriend in outrage.

'Can you believe this?' I'd say, gesturing at the latest outrageous quote.

'Yeah, I can,' he'd say. 'It's a bishop.'

Why did this rankle so much? I was hardly surprised that the Church was against abortion. And anyway, I had no right to critique how senior clerics were running their Church. I had abandoned faith entirely more than a decade before, one of the thousands of young Irish people that the institution was haemorrhaging in the wake of endemic abuse scandals and a refusal to let go of archaic prejudices. The popular view among people my age is that the Church is an obsolete institution that should have the minimal influence possible on Irish society. Identifying yourself as non-religious is a virtue signal, possibly in the way that identifying as Catholic would have been in an earlier time. If anything, I was diametrically, completely and utterly anti-Catholic.

Well, people contradict themselves all the time. We have different versions of ourselves for different parts of life. It has taken me a long time to understand that focusing on the things that people are best known for can be the worst way to try to know them.

As the referendum campaign moved with increasing intensity towards voting day, these complicated feelings about the Church were growing inside me. I was becoming disproportionately annoyed at the things that senior clerics and other Catholics were saying. A lot of young women my age were paying very little attention to priests' and bishops' musings on reproductive healthcare. Many thought that what the Church had to say on repeal was inconsequential, that it would have zero influence on most voters. I must have had higher standards for clerics than I realised. I thought what they had to say was important, and it was aggravating me that their message seemed so wrong. In the final week of the campaign, I had to stay home from work after waking up with period pain so bad it seemed vengeful. It was the Monday before the vote and I was lying in bed listening to the radio. A politician who had always clearly wedded his anti-abortion views to his faith was doing an interview calling for a No vote. He was asked about women who had to travel for terminations and how that would continue if the Eighth Amendment remained in the constitution. In response, the politician decided to make a point about different people going to different jurisdictions to benefit from different laws. For example, he explained, many companies decided to come to Ireland to benefit from our low corporate tax rate.

Sometimes people talk about how sex feels better when you're on drugs. I think that rage feels better when you're on your period – you really get the full benefit of the emotion. I was lying there in bed, crippled with cramps and fizzing with fury. Corporation tax? Far harsher and more controversial things were said about women over the course of that referendum, but the cold comparison between women looking for reproductive healthcare and greedy inanimate international corporations incensed me the most. Maybe it's because I was, at that moment, enduring the painful tyranny of my own constant egg production, but the comments and the whole referendum suddenly made me feel very out of control. I felt hyper-conscious of being born in a body that *could* be pregnant, and even though I could make the choice that this politician wanted, I still wasn't legally offered the chance to make it. Most of all, I was furious that this was the voice of a 'Catholic' No voter. It did not sound like a very Christian way to talk about women. And it was in total anger that I finally found clarity: I was annoyed at the suggestion that the only Catholic vote was a No vote. I thought this was wrong and unfair. A Catholic voting Yes in line with their own conscience and their sense of compassion (a Christian quality) wasn't just conceivable, it was precisely what was going to happen for thousands of people on 25 May – the day of the vote. But why would I care about that? Because, I realised, the reasons that I had for voting Yes were Catholic ones.

You become the person that you are for lots of different reasons. There's your personality, for a start. There's the way your parents raised you. There are formative experiences as a child that shape the way you think and feel. And there is religion.

Every single moral lesson I had as a child was tethered to religion. I learned the difference between right and wrong, but I also learned that doing the wrong thing would not just be morally wrong, it would also be a disappointment to God. I am sure that other religions give people a similar structure to their lives, but I can only speak from my own experience. I grew up understanding Catholicism to be a moral code and an ethical guide. It taught me early on about the importance of looking after others and being kind to people. This is exactly what women who make the difficult decision to access an abortion need.

When I was starting out as a journalist, I wrote a lot about the Eighth Amendment and the cruel and inflexible consequences of it. I also wrote a lot about bad things that anti-abortion activists did in the name of their Catholic cause – like setting up fake crisis-pregnancy agencies to dupe women and scare them away from an abortion. I was about 24 years old when I started writing these articles. Being a young woman covering reproductive rights makes people instinctively see you as some sort of unreliable narrator. This doesn't seem to happen in other cases. Reporters have highlighted and reported on the tracker-mortgage scandal from one clear side or perspective, but they never seem to be seen as unreliable, despite the fact that they live in houses. I can't think of many men who were told they were too biased to cover the referendum, despite abortion being one issue that almost everyone has a view on. Covering the citizens' assembly, I watched a very senior male reporter make emotional demands for the entire transcripts from interviews with women who had spoken about their crisis pregnancies to the assembly to be made available to him. The press officer from the citizens' assembly explained that that couldn't be done because it would reveal the identities of the women, who had chosen to remain anonymous.

'I'd get them if it was a tribunal,' he raged.

'But this isn't a tribunal,' the press officer said. 'Nobody has committed a crime.'

Even within Irish journalism, older male colleagues often suggested that I was biased for writing about the flaws of the Eighth Amendment. I thought that pointing out laws that do not work and campaigning for them to change was one of the most basic aspects of print journalism, and always had been.

Women reporters who wrote about the Eighth Amendment were often deemed biased and were savaged on the internet. Years later, I still brace myself whenever anything good happens – a new job, a big story – because there is a cohort of anti-abortion activists who hate me so much they'll use it as a chance to abuse me again. It was decided that I was tenaciously, dangerously pro-choice. I was dismissed as an extreme feminazi who put so much store in personal autonomy that I would sanction abortion up until birth if I had my way. Nobody bothered to ask what my own view was. I think it was decided that the thing I was best known for writing about was the best way to know what my views were.

I have always believed that life begins at conception, and everything I wrote about abortion law has enhanced that belief rather than shaken it. The more I sat in Dáil committees or citizens' assembly meetings listening to details about the process of abortion, the surer I became that there is a life there.

Allegedly feminist arguments about a foetus just being a 'lump of cells' would leave me cold. If there wasn't a life there, abortion law wouldn't dominate internationally as one of the most controversial and emotional social and political issues in the world. I also had the privilege during all this work of learning a lot more about human life in general, the different whys and hows and reasons and instincts that lie behind every termination.

If there is anything I have learned from the women who have told me their stories, it's that nobody can truly predict what would happen were they to be faced with a crisis pregnancy. You can only know what your beliefs are and assume that they would influence your choice, but they may not ultimately decide it. My personal beliefs lead me to think that I would not choose to terminate a pregnancy, but that's an easy thing to say from my luxurious position of never having had to decide.

I know that I must be pro-choice because I trust people to make a choice that I believe I would not. I find the necessity for abortion sad, and I would prefer to live in a society where a law legalising it was not required. I have heard women eloquently rail against the suggestion that abortion is always difficult or always a hard choice. They point out that for some women it's an easy decision, and not as emotive as common conceptions would suggest. I think those women are right. It's difficult for me, but it's not difficult for everyone.

I'm not anti-abortion but I am pro-life, and women have lives as well. I think you can believe that life begins at conception but know that it's wrong to try to vindicate that right at any cost. Values aren't worth anything when we use them as arbitrary rules for black and white situations. I wanted to vote Yes because the Eighth Amendment did not work: it was designed to stop abortion; it had failed. Worse than that, its mangled attempt to force women to continue pregnancies through law had caused more harm than good. Women had been abandoned and made to suffer, stigmatised and sent away. I wanted to vote Yes out of a sense of compassion for them.

Yes, the need for abortion makes me sad, but when I think how many abortions have been carried out in Ireland in the days and months since the law changed, it is not a source of sadness for me. I have to trust all those women.

They know better than me what was right for them. I had to choose Yes for the greater good.

I voted Yes with my conscience, based on values that I now know are Christian ones: compassion, empathy and understanding. It made me bitter to think of all those priests and the conservative Catholic commentators who told Catholics not to vote with their conscience. Ignore your conscience? I thought Catholicism was supposed to be sociology for optimists – based heavily on the assumption that people are fundamentally good. The ability to be good and do good is in all of us already. But the Church wanted us to ignore what our conscience told us was the right thing to do. No, those priests seemed to say, we'll decide. Father knows best.

The Friday of the vote came and went. In the end 1,429,981 people, over 66 per cent, voted Yes to lift Ireland's ban on abortion. I imagine a lot of those people, like me, had had a Catholic education. I expected the relief, but I didn't expect the sense of patriotism. I felt like I could love Ireland without qualifications or conditions.

I left Dublin Castle after filing my last article on the result. I had wanted to be in every part of the courtyard at once, desperate to absorb every part of this momentous day and commit it to memory. Me and a few other reporters stumbled into a pub across the road. Later on, a few drinks in, someone was holding court. 'This isn't a Catholic country anymore,' they said. Oh, but it is, I thought. This is the most Catholic thing we've done in ages. Usually, when Ireland is described as a 'Catholic country' it's in a pejorative way. A lot of people who voted Yes weren't Catholic, and may not even have been religious. The country voting in favour of an approach that was more compassionate and understanding felt to me like a country that was very much in line with Catholic values, which I was starting to feel were very important to me.

After the referendum, the feelings about the Church stayed. Quietly and unexpectedly, they would start to dominate my thoughts at random moments. I felt like I was in a state of shock. The sense of realisation was slow but potent. I was missing something, and maybe I had wasted years not realising it was missing. I had always assumed that the things I was passionate about – marriage equality, women's rights – were things I cared about despite being raised Catholic. I bought the conservative Catholic think tank's portrayal of people like me as annoying social justice warriors who are fundamental enemies of the Church. But maybe those causes were things I cared about because I was raised Catholic? And if that was true, maybe I cared about faith more than I thought?

——— ⚜ ———

Catholicism was knitted into my life from the very start. I remember the picture of the Sacred Heart that hung in my house so vividly I could draw it from memory. All around the house were little statues of St Anthony and St Francis. (My dad used to make them dance and joke that it was an All Saints gig.) Every now and then neighbours would show up with a mysterious box with what looked like a rag inside it, and it would be our job to mind it for a few days. These were alleged relics that were passed around like chain letters.

I remember being in school in Touraneena, where I grew up, and Fr Kelleher, the parish priest, coming in to talk to us. I had assumed that priests had some magical powers, or else they wouldn't have such an important job – the same way the Santa you visit in SuperValu before Christmas is not actually the real deal but a magical disciple who has a direct line back to the North Pole to report any misdemeanours. I thought Fr Kelleher could read my mind, and I always panicked when he came into the classroom because I would immediately be unable to think of anything other than my most recent fight with my sister.

For my first confession, I felt that none of my misdeeds were good enough for the sacrament of penance, so I embellished. I lied and told Fr Kelleher that I had stolen some penny sweets. This sparked a manic shame spiral as soon as I left the confession box and realised that I had now lied to a priest, which was probably the worst thing I had ever done. If there hadn't been a queue of other children behind me, I would have burst back through the little fabric curtain in tears and pleaded for clemency.

I was around nine when I was granted the prestige of being an altar girl, something my mother's generation had never been allowed to do because it had only been for boys. I still remember the smell of the red robe we'd pull over our heads in the sacristy, with a smaller white one to go on top. Being an altar server was very cool but, unfortunately, for very secular and material reasons. When people died, altar servers would get the morning off school for the burial. Afterwards, you'd be given a few pound coins to buy sweets in the shop next to the church. You could then strut around the playground, swinging a jelly worm like it was a status symbol.

The worst part of the gig was Holy Thursday, when the priest would have to wash the altar servers' feet the way Jesus did with the twelve disciples. Mine would have already been scrubbed to the point of erasure by my mother, who was afraid of the priest judging anything-less-than-immaculate feet. I remember clutching the sides of one of the wooden seats that we sat on at either side of the altar and trying to point my toes to make my foot look dainty and elegant while it was being washed in front of the whole parish. The priest would never dry your foot properly. It was more of a decorative pat with the towel, the way you're supposed to dry yourself after a spray tan. But I would sit diligent and still for the rest of the mass, pretending my foot wasn't soaking through my sock.

I remember once praying for a kitten and then being astounded by the power of God when a stray cat on our farm got pregnant. And I liked praying. I liked talking to God in my head. I liked believing.

But then I grew older, and everything I knew about Catholicism was eclipsed by everything I learned about the Catholic Church. Magdalene laundries, mother-and-baby homes, endless news reports about unthinkable abuse. By the time I was a teenager, people my age and older had left the faith in their droves. 'Catholic Ireland' became an adage, referring to a dark, backwards and shameful time. Being Irish Catholic, something that had been so hard won, became something to repent for. Most of the societal good done by Catholicism was erased in the minds of the public, or effectively cancelled out by the heinous things that the Church did as well. You know what's coming when you see the word 'Catholic' on a newspaper front page: it is nothing good. I was raised to understand that the clergy were people who had made major sacrifices for the sake of their vocation. They were supposed to be role models in morality. Now, people say things like 'not all' priests are bad, as if finding a good person of the cloth is a pleasant surprise.

Obviously, this is why I left. It's why loads of people left. But after repeal, I started going over things in my head. Leaving was an act of protest, but I incorrectly assumed it was a form of punishment for the Church as well. I used to relish the fact that the clerical hierarchy would have to notice the depleting and dwindling numbers at mass and realise that their power was gone. But even without the power and the prestige and the status and even the trust, the Church still had something much, much more precious than we did. We all left, and we let the Church keep the faith. Literally.

By leaving, I and a lot of other people let the Church steal faith away. What a major heist. It's a big existential loss, but it also means being deprived of the everyday things that are as close to tangible as you're ever going to get with faith. Going to mass for the ritual and the community. Like having a clear guide for living a better life. A lot of people lost the beauty of private prayer: having someone to talk to in times of crisis or someone to thank in times of joy. It also meant losing a layer of beauty in the world. Everything is in lower definition – to me anyway – when you can't see God in things like nature or other people's kindness. Worst of all, it meant losing the invaluable comfort of knowing it's not the end when somebody dies. Thinking about that one almost makes me cry. Faith is so precious. A lot of conscientious people lost their faith, and a lot of people who did damage to the Church got to keep it. That doesn't seem fair.

When something like prayer has been there for your entire life, you don't think too much about what it really is that you're doing. Like a lot of people my age, I had left the Church a long time ago. By the end of my teens, I thought there was nothing in the Church for me. I lost all respect for the Church. I stopped going to church and before I realised it had happened, I was out of the religion completely. But I had kept talking to God. (Though, I am embarrassed to admit, this had become less and less frequent as time went on.) In desperate moments of heartache, of course I had turned to prayer again. When I thought back on those moments, I realised that each time I had believed wholly and unconditionally in what I was doing: I never doubted that God was real or that prayer worked. I had not stopped believing, but I had forgotten that I still believed.

Once you realise that you're missing it, it is almost impossible to go on without it. But this is not a simple story about a prodigal daughter. Everything that drove me away from the Church in the first place is still real, whether you believe in God or not. I have major problems with the Church's views on women and LGBT+ people, and the way that it turned its back on child abuse to protect itself.

I am about to turn 30, and I will never be able to get back the last decade, where I didn't engage with what I believed in. I really don't want to go into the next decade without it. But I don't want my return to the Church to mean I'm giving my tacit support to misogynistic or homophobic views. It would be selfish to use faith for my own benefit while turning a blind eye to all of the terrible things done in the name of the religion.

The crisis of faith was the easy part. The crisis of conscience was much harder. I had to figure out how much I really wanted to go back to the Church. I also had to ask if leaving it in the first place had been a mistake.

Chapter 2

The church was open and dry – that's the only reason I went inside.

This was the first time I'd seen this church, even though I'd passed it often enough. It sat right in the centre of an extremely busy high street, flanked on either end with lush boutiques and pubs. I wonder how people saw the church's prominent position: defiant or desperate? Maybe people liked having it there, as a quiet statement against the excess all around it. Or maybe some people thought its presence in such a central part of the town made it a monument to a different country.

I was there to visit a priest in the parochial house next door, but I was uncharacteristically early. Over the last few weeks and months, my crisis of faith had moved on from the initial Catholic-curiosity to what I like to call my 'Carmela Soprano complex'. I didn't want to be someone who just used religion to assuage my guilt about the less Christian aspects of my life – like how Carmela remains utterly devout to Catholicism, but never thinks too hard about where Tony gets those lovely mink coats from. I don't want to go through life like a mob wife, using religion in a superficial way – going about my days complicit in sin while I cook delicious lasagnes. I know that religion can appeal to my selfish side – everybody wants to feel like they're a good person, and if you have faith, maybe that gives you the quiet reassurance that you are. Letting everyone know that you are devoted to what is basically a charter for goodness is the ultimate virtue signal. It's attractive to the narcissist in me as well. If you're yearning for meaning or purpose, you could easily use religion to reassure you about your place in the cosmos. It feels good to think that our little existences are part of a plan too grand for all of us to understand. I was trying hard to think about finding faith again as carefully as I could, to make sure I wasn't just using those parts of it to make myself feel better.

As if that wasn't neurotic enough, while I worried about whether I was good enough for the Church, I was also worrying whether the Church was good enough for anyone. Based on its treatment of abuse survivors, women and LGBT+ people, I wasn't even sure if going back to Catholicism was the Christian thing to do.

I wanted to find a reason to go back, rather than an excuse. It was exhausting trying to mull this over, and I think my boyfriend was fed up with the existential questions. And if I have learned anything from *The Sopranos* it's that if you're not talking to a therapist, you should probably be talking to a priest.

So with half an hour to spare before I met the priest and no sign of the miserable rain abating, I went into the church. It was like the Tardis from *Dr Who*. The plain exterior concealed a stunning interior, with a yawning roof that I was sure had to be much higher than the building was on the outside. It was painted in deep blues and rich indigos. It smelled like incense and must, the same smell I used to get when I pulled on my altar-server gowns.

I was standing in a large, quiet hallway. It had a tiled floor so polished it looked like a still lake. As I walked deeper, I saw an alcove to my right containing a wooden confession box with a rich, red curtain. Beyond an arch ahead of me was the chapel. A row of seats was pressed near the back of the chapel, and I sat down. About two metres ahead of me were the last of the rows of pews. It was busier than I'd thought it would be for the middle of the day on a weekday. Almost a dozen people were dotted throughout the church, immersed in prayer. A young man in a tracksuit was sitting three rows from the back. There were a lot of middle-aged women. An older man came in and sat down in the last pew, in front of me. The air was thick with silence. It was so still it was like time had stopped.

There was a physical gap between me and the people praying in the pews, but in other ways I was already a million miles away from them. I felt like there was a big, thick glass wall between us. They were all lost in something that I couldn't really imagine having. Without the weird combination of both the spectacle and monotony of mass, this quiet church felt much more beautiful than ones I'd been in before. More spiritual – that's the word I'm looking for. I saw that one of the women had some Brown Thomas bags resting next to her as she kneeled; another had a huge reusable bag of groceries on the pew beside her. They had broken the ordinariness of their days to come in here for something, and I wondered what it was. This room of strangers praying together was intimate and anonymous at the same time – there was no way to know who was saying a prayer of thanksgiving, who was saying a prayer in desperation. Maybe some were just saying a prayer out of habit.

I suddenly felt overwhelmed with emotion. Was there such a thing as a religious placebo? You see people who desperately want to fall in love, will themselves into it all the time. If I came into a church looking to find faith, could I trick myself into thinking I had? But the problem was this didn't feel that good. I realised the quietness I was feeling in the church was peace, and of course that felt nice. But I had a bad feeling in my chest too, an emotional pang. I felt intrusive watching these people pray because I felt that maybe I was much further from having what they had than I had realised. It was like Catholic FOMO.

I got up and left, quickly. When I emerged outside, the priest was standing next door at the parochial house, beaming down at his feet. As he saw me walking towards him, he gestured down at the ground in glee.

'I just came out here to meet you, and look at what I found! A €2! Isn't that wonderful? Isn't that a great sign?' I was immediately charmed.

He led me inside the parochial house, through a warren of staircases and tiny rooms and corridors until it felt like we'd looped back around to the front of the house in a big horseshoe. He led me into a huge dining room with a large mahogany table, and both of us perched on chairs at the top of it. He kept offering me cake until I gave in.

I used to think politicians had a monopoly on wanting to talk 'off the record', and then I started hanging out with priests. The Irish clergy must have everything it needs to stage a tiny revolution if all of the priests in favour of reform would just start talking to each other. Or at least start talking about it out loud.

This priest didn't want to be named. He talked about the cruel and often nonsensical inflexibility of the Church. He told me how he broke some of its arbitrary rules every week when he gave communion to his divorced brother. He mentioned clericalism; all the people who had climbed the greasy pole and were using the religion to serve themselves, rather than God.

He talked about people like Cardinal Farrell, the Irish Vatican official probably best known now for being the man who barred Mary McAleese from speaking in the Vatican for International Women's Day.

The priest pulled up a picture of the cardinal on his phone. The senior Vatican official was swaddled in rich red robes, extravagant to the point of ridiculousness. As he sat on a little throne, the long fabric gathered in bundles at his feet like a red velvet Viennetta.

'So you see, I'm up against it, the Pope is up against it,' he said, and then he gestured towards the picture on his phone. 'Jesus is up against it.'

We talked for a long time. I had come armed with some pretty unreasonable demands: I wanted him to give me straight answers to my big, esoteric questions about whether or not it was right to go back to the Church. Every time I asked, he would masterfully turn the conversation back on me.

I wanted to know if I was a hypocrite if I went back.

'What do you think, yourself?' the priest said. 'This desire to go back, what does it feel like?'

I was dumbstruck. I didn't know how to put words on what I was feeling, so I said nothing.

After a few seconds of silence, the priest spoke again. 'A place where you have to obey all these rules you don't agree with, that's not there anymore, anyway. I mean, most of the people who go to the churches voted for marriage equality, in conscience, that's the bottom line,' he said.

'But, sure, isn't that the crowd that Jesus hung around with when he was around? And the people he fell out with were the rule-makers. So if you're in this crowd, you're in good company.

'Who's to say, when it comes down to it? Who's to say what's right or wrong? It's your conscience. The old stuff is cold and lifeless and kind of dark. So back to that question, what do you think yourself? Why do you want to come back?'

'I think I would like it,' I said eventually. 'I think I would really like to come back. Like, I was so jealous of the people next door even before I came in –'

'Here?' he interjected, gesturing at the church next door. I nodded.

'Jealous,' he said, and then he went quiet for a moment. 'That sounds like it's something you're lonesome for, something you're missing.'

I tried to say 'yes' but it only came out in a whisper. I was horrified to feel emotion start to bloom at the back of my throat. Before I knew what was happening, I was blinking back tears.

'Yeah,' the priest said. 'And, without getting too pious, I believe that is a gift from God to you. That sense that He's not finished with you yet. You are missing Him, or you are missing. You arrived half an hour before the meeting. Is that an accident? That you find yourself there? And then the feeling: what have they got that I haven't? And that you're kind of longing for almost, is it?'

I don't know if you have ever cried in front of a priest, but I would heartily endorse the experience. By this point, tears were streaming down my face. I had been completely ambushed by emotion. I had no idea why I was finding this so upsetting, but the tears felt pretty cathartic. As for the priest, he couldn't have been less fazed. There was none of the excruciating social awkwardness that usually ruins a perfectly good cry. He reacted as though bursting into tears was one of the most natural things in the world – which it is. It's the response of someone who must see people cry a lot, who has probably had to pull people through some terrible anguish.

It was true, I was longing for something. I think I was crying tears of realisation.

The priest just kept talking me through it, while his face wrinkled in concentration. He nodded slowly, as though what was dawning on me was dawning on him too.

'Something is starting to connect,' he said, and he pointed at his head. 'It's not up here anymore. You're jealous of those people. That's a strong word. It doesn't capture it too much but it's like you're ... maybe He's saying something to you there. And He might be feeling the same thing,' he said. 'Some sort of connection with you there. It works both ways.'

I know how this sounds. When the priest says this, I believe it. Really, truly, devoutly believe it. Because I felt it, and it felt real. But I can appreciate how, for some people, the suggestion that I just happened to have a timely brush with God right at the point where I was having a crisis of faith may be veering into the realms of the unbelievable.

When I was younger, my mother was as unwavering in her belief in Jesus Christ as she was in her belief in ghosts. I was raised to believe that ghosts were a little hindrance we all just had to deal with – an unfortunate fact of life, like ants. As a child, I used to lie poker-still in my bed, listening to the unearthly wailing outside and waiting with sad resignation for a banshee to come get me. I was well into my twenties before I realised I had been lying in terror inside my house while two foxes had been innocuously having sex outside it. In our isolated rural home, I had plenty of brushes with the paranormal. Glasses would break, pictures would fall off the wall, doors would slam – your basic poltergeist starter pack. My mother would comfort me, but never once entertained the idea of shielding me from what she saw as the inconvenient reality: I lived in a haunted house and there was nothing anybody could do about it.

As a teenager, I would watch with exasperation as my mam would solicit the services of anyone who ever appeared on TV3 claiming to be able to talk to dead people. And in the early 2000s, all TV3 seemed to be was mid-morning interviews with people who claimed to be able to talk to dead people. A carousel of incense-yielding men would come to our house and do something weird to try to get rid of our ghosts, to my perpetual adolescent mortification. One of them claimed that there was a spirit in my room. I watched with bored irritation as he claimed to shoo the ghost into the corner, above my wastepaper basket.

'You can feel the heat of it, if you like,' he said.

I complied, sticking my hand into the corner and feeling absolutely nothing.

'Wow, yeah,' I said.

'No, not there,' he said, looking at me like I was some sort of idiot. 'Here.'

He moved my arm up a few inches, and I withdrew it in shock straight away.

It was as if I'd put my hand straight into the steam from a boiling kettle. I stared at him in horror.

'I told you,' he said with a shrug.

Once, the local parish priest even came over to our house to do a Ouija board. I am certainly not the person to be pulling anyone up on not strictly adhering to the rules of the Catholic Church, but I am sure that fraternising with the occult would have been a big no-no with the bishop.

I often roll out these spooky stories from my childhood in dramatic retellings for friends in the pub, and my boyfriend will sit and watch while wearing the face of someone who is sadly adjusting to the fact that the person they love has lost the plot. When we hear a bump in bed at night, I'll turn to him and give him a knowing look. 'Ghost,' I'll say, and he'll look back at me with a mix of pity and confusion. Sometimes I feel like he treats me and my penchant for spirits the way everyone else treats Leonardo Di Caprio on *Shutter Island*: with reluctant humouring.

What I'm trying to say is that I am well used to seeing the kinds of incredulous faces people might wear on hearing about my religious experience in the church that day. What I am also trying to say is that I am predisposed to believing in magic, and possibly the only time in my life that will have any real value for me is now. I don't know why we don't spend more time talking about the best part of faith: the magic bit. It doesn't matter what kind of Catholic you are – stern, pious, kind, serious or fundamentalist – all of us have to believe in magic if we're going to believe in God.

I don't mean the controversial magic trick with the bread, or even the immaculate conception. I mean prayer: the most basic part of the faith, the part that anyone can do, is based on magic. You have to suspend your disbelief and simply trust that there is something there in the ether, listening to you, before you can pray properly. This is the part of the faith that people like to ridicule the most, with trite observations about grown adults talking to an imaginary man in the sky. But it seems silly to me to apply logic to something that feels so inexplicable and intangible and mysterious. It's like trying to use an abacus to count all the stars in a galaxy. In religion class, when I was younger, I remember a teacher explaining 'unconditional belief' to me – that you can't apply the usual terms and conditions and caveats to your belief in God as you would to other normal human things. And I don't think religion demands total blind faith. If you have faith, you know it's real because you can feel something. It's just hard to explain what that something is. I understand if people don't get that.

So when the priest suggested that my feeling of longing was a kind of conversation between me and God, I believed him. We both sat in a comfortable silence for a long time.

'You know,' he said finally, 'that's a pretty profound experience. How many churches would you just walk in and out of and think nothing? But today, you see people going in and out and you don't know what's going on with them either. They're lighting candles for thanksgiving, for heartbreak, even for a bit of peace. It's the beauty of the place. But what happened with you there is, I think, lovely. Cherish that little desire that's in you, the longing in you that's not being met with the biro or whatever you do for the paper.'

'But,' I said, 'would I be welcomed back?'

'What do you think? I would welcome you back with my arms open – because I don't think you've far to come. I could imagine the Lord would be saying to you, certainly, come back.'

For the sake of the cynics, I asked him if he thought I could have just conjured this experience from my own mind – willed myself into an emotional moment in the church because it's what I wanted to happen.

'You can't make faith happen just because you want it to,' he said. 'Faith is a gift. You have no evidence for it, and that is a gift. It puts colour in life. It's mysterious but beautiful.'

I left and started walking towards the train station. I wanted to call someone to tell them about what happened, but I didn't know how I'd explain it. I thought about the questions I'd gone in there with and felt like a bit of an eejit.

My first attempts to figure out how to get my religion back had been so cold and academic – arguing with myself over and back about the rights and the wrongs. Those moral quandaries are still important, but I was in such a rush to get them answered I had skipped past the more foundational questions. Now I knew one thing for sure: I definitely believed. That was as good a reason to investigate going back to the Church as any.

Chapter 3

I'm flat on my stomach under my bed. My nose is pressed into the wooden floorboards, and my clothes are covered in dust. My hand is extended to the farthest, darkest corners, brushing along the skirting boards, looking for change. I'm 17 years old. Me and my friends were out the night before, and one of them stayed with her boyfriend. They had sex and she needed to get emergency contraception. At this point in time – Ireland, 2008 – that also meant she needed about €130.

When I was a teenager, the mornings after were sometimes nicer than the nights before. Everyone would emerge from the beds of friends and boyfriends and start coordinating a way to collect cars that had been discarded in town. Fiestas, Ibizas and Corollas all doubled up as places to predrink, once we'd parked up anywhere that wouldn't clamp us overnight. On Sunday mornings we'd breeze into each other's houses unannounced and uninvited, crawl into beds and start gossiping. My house was the closest to town so I always had loads of visits from the girls, which I loved.

This particular morning I had heard the front door slam, a generic greeting from my mother in the kitchen ('Well, had ye a good night?') and then footsteps pounding up the stairs. That's when I found out we needed to sort the pill for one of the girls.

My attitude to sex was so old-fashioned when I was young. As three of us sat on my bed and upended our clutch bags onto the sheets, I felt weird about what we were doing. Back then, emergency contraception was not available over the counter in Ireland. That would not happen until I was 20 years old. So you had to pay for a GP appointment, which was €50, plus the price of the pill itself, which back then was €80. That was the kind of money that we had to scramble together. All our handbags were offering up was lint and lipstick, so I tried under the bed. Pulling a €2 coin towards me, I didn't feel judgemental and I didn't feel embarrassed, but I did feel like I was doing something wrong. Not in a morally anguished kind of way, just in the way teenagers casually do so many things that they know to be wrong.

Nobody has ever sat me down and tried to teach me to hate women, never mind using religion to do it. The way I felt – the way loads of us felt – about sex and shame and women was much more complicated than simply claiming that the Church tried to turn misogyny into a Catholic virtue. Sometimes what you're not taught can be more defining than what you are taught. When it came to sex, and particularly women having sex, there was a huge vacuum. Shame filled it. The wrongness of female sexuality was never set down in anything as black and white as a commandment. It was more like something in the atmosphere that touched everything, including how I was feeling about emergency contraception.

We scraped the money together. We didn't need to talk about why she needed it. At that point, though we didn't know it, we were still over a decade away from Ireland lifting its near-ban on abortion. Obviously, if scraping together €130 posed a problem then covering the cost of travelling to the UK would have been almost impossible.

Because it was a Sunday, the three of us had to drive to the out-of-hours CareDoc – as if having sex had been some goofy, unexpected accident. I felt like we were doing something clandestine. That must be why the 'they' that run the world when you're a teenager made it hard to access the morning-after pill, I thought, to make it seem illicit. After my friend went in, I was still sitting with this weird discomfort. Why did this feel so awkward? Why were we all acting so embarrassed? Where was this shame coming from?

I know that 17 is quite an old age to get to without fully understanding how the world sees and treats women. There were good and bad reasons for why I was so sheltered, which I'll get to later. My friend got into the car and put on her seat belt.

'The nurse was a bitch,' she said.

'What?' I said.

'She just spoke to me like I was a slut.'

The word 'slut' stung. It wasn't said about me or to me, but it still hurt. These stings had happened a few times now, and each time they'd felt worse. About a year and a half before this, I'd been caught underage drinking by the guards. As in vomiting in the garda station, liaison officer assigned, your mother's basic nightmare. The bollocking was phenomenal. I was upstairs one night when a load of relatives – who were thrilled, *thrilled* with the absolute scandal of it all – were down in the living room clucking with my parents about how much worse it could have been. My hypothetical death was deemed very tragic. But what's worse than that? Sure, I could have gotten pregnant as well.

'Well,' I heard a male relative say in a loaded tone, 'we're not out of the woods yet.'

That was the first sting. I was only 15 and it was the first time I'd heard someone talk about my body like that. As if it was this petulant thing that could mortify me and everyone who belonged to me at any moment by deciding to be pregnant. It made me feel embarrassed and afraid of what being a girl meant.

Around the time of the trip to get the pill, I'd had a row with a boyfriend. I can't remember what about, but I remember that halfway through he abandoned whatever his argument was and decided to just attack. 'Anyway, what was the fucking story with your skirt last night?' he'd texted, berating me about how short it was and what that meant and what people would have said. I felt like I'd been slapped. Like the pregnancy comment or the 'slut' word, it is obviously nowhere near the worst thing that's happened to me under the banner of sexism. The only reason any of those things are significant is because they happened at a time when I still had no reason to expect them to. I'm not sure if other women have had moments like that, but for me the realisation was like an adolescent version of finding out about Santa Claus. It's the genuine 'red pill' moment that men's rights activists try to convince themselves into experiencing.

Once I understood sexism properly, I felt so mad about the wrongness of it. This pushed me away from the Church in my late teens with the force of two opposing magnets. There was such a clear conflict between what I knew to be right or wrong and what I had been taught – implicitly or otherwise – to be right or wrong. Catholicism – the faith – isn't misogynistic. The Catholic Church is. The Church's most controversial policies, like its views on women, are often reflected in the place where it still wields much power and influence in Ireland: education.

———— ✿ ————

If you'd like to create a total frenzy around sex, might I recommend a Catholic education for your young and impressionable adolescent?

When I was in school, there was little to no sex education, and from what I can see, in some schools not a lot has
changed since. Entire swathes of our teenage school-going
population are not taught about contraception or the existence of LGBT+ people because of the Catholic ethos of their
schools. Those who rail against reform and argue in favour
of 'keeping Catholic schools Catholic' will say that this is an
educational choice that Catholic parents should be allowed
to make on the basis of their own beliefs. The problem is that
many parents, Catholic or otherwise, do not have a choice.
A Catholic school might be the only one available to you.
Even before you get to the obvious wrong of non-religious
families being forced to choose a Catholic education, there
is also little scope for Catholic parents who might want a
modern and normal sex education for their children.

Everything I learned about sex and gender, I learned
from my convent school. What a trip that was. I attended
Ard Scoil na nDeise in Dungarvan, County Waterford. It's
an all-girls school based in a former convent, which is, of
course, yards away from an all-boys school run by the
Christian Brothers. Irish Catholic schools tend to divide you
up by binary gender right when puberty hits. This created
a mystique around teenage boys, which I think served them
in an undeservedly flattering way.

I wonder if the refusal to acknowledge LGBT+ people
led my school to believe that everyone was not just heterosexual, but tenaciously heterosexual. Girls and boys were

to be kept apart at all costs. In Transition Year, there was a tradition that we adorably thought was very egalitarian and radical. Our school, which had at least three massive kitchens for home economics classes, would let Transition Year students from the Christian Brothers come and learn to cook for a couple of weeks. The boys' school, naturally, did not have any kitchens. Later in the term we would then swap, and me and the rest of the girls would be briefly let into their woodwork studio and the care of a harassed-looking teacher who obviously hated every minute of this social experiment. Great care was taken to make sure our paths never crossed with the boys. We'd be shooed down the road to the boys' school and escorted in quickly as if we were a herd of precious geishas. Unfortunately, the boys' culinary skills did nothing to shatter gender stereotypes. So despite the best efforts of the teachers, we'd all end up standing outside bashfully staring at each other after the school was evacuated en masse following the screams of another fire alarm.

Because of these intense conditions in our school, the presence of even the most underwhelming male could cause a hormonal furore. There was a substantial uptake of higher-level physics in my year, largely because the teacher was a man who was also very nice. This phenomenon must not have escaped the notice of some Catholic 'educational' groups, especially the ones who were preaching about chastity. Sex sells, even when what you're selling is not having sex.

One day in school, we were all sent to the junior hall for a talk. I must have been about 14 or 15. When we arrived, dozens of chairs had been laid out in a big semicircle. An extremely conservative Catholic group called Pure in Heart had come to speak to us. And they had deployed the most potent weapon they had: moderately attractive young men. There was a bang of PG-rated American summer-camp guides off them. Think of the kind of person you could imagine saying 'gee willikers!'

For reasons I'd rather not dwell on, I was selected by an earnest and floppy-haired fella as a volunteer for a very important demonstration. I was brought to the front of the room and told to roll up the sleeve of my thick royal-blue school jumper. A roll of Sellotape was produced with a flourish.

After asking me my name, the youth asked us all to imagine a scenario when 'Ellen meets a guy at a disco and they have sex.' Fantasy fiction, I think it's called. On the word 'sex', he put a strip of Sellotape on my arm and then pulled it off.

'Then,' he said, 'imagine Ellen goes to college and meets someone there, and they have sex?' He stuck the strip back on my arm. *Whoop* went the Sellotape, as it was whipped off my arm again. We went through the scenario once more, this time with an imaginary suitor that I met at my first job. (So far, I was finding this story absolutely thrilling. Imagine! Three people wanting to have sex with me!)

'Now, imagine Ellen and I meet, and we fall in love,' he said. 'We're the real deal. She's the love of my life.' This, as far as my fraternising with men had gone at that point, felt breathtakingly explicit.

He stuck his arm out and, using the same tired strip of Sellotape, tried to 'tape' the two of us together.

'And now,' he said, gesturing meaningfully as the tape hung on pathetically, 'it doesn't work.'

I didn't have a clue what this meant. Even now, I'm still not 100 per cent sure. While I've admittedly suffered from a complete dearth of any formal sex education, even I know that sex doesn't stop working after a specific number of partners. However, when you're talking to teenage girls who know absolutely nothing about sex, vague implications can speak volumes. Terrified of exposing my cluelessness, I tried to adopt a sage and meaningful facial expression.

'But of course,' I hoped my face said. 'The sex, it won't work.'

Everybody else nodded as well, with the same 'ah, but of course!' looks on their faces. At this point, we were already intoxicated by the thrill of having some young men pay close and respectful attention to us. But they were saving the *pièce de résistance* for the end. In his concluding talk, when I was safely back in my seat, my adhesive attacker told us a story. He told us how he really had met the love of his life, this amazing girl who he was head over heels for. They had, of course, not had sex but enjoyed an incredible bond.

'And now,' he said with a dramatic pause, as if it had just that second occurred to him, 'I'm going to ask that girl to marry me.'

It had the desired reaction. The entire hall of girls cooed and sighed in wild appreciation. Those cute hoors knew well the power of a cheesy heteronormative engagement story.

A couple of years later, we had a talk from a nun. That wasn't unusual. The subject was missionary work that she'd been doing, but she digressed and told us an anecdote about a girl who lived in New York who had experienced a miracle. This lady was going home on the subway one night when a man tried to attack her. At the last second, he stopped. Looking behind the young woman, he appeared to see something that spooked him. When the girl turned around, the Virgin Mary was standing behind her.

As far as tales of bodacious saints go, this one was already pretty solid. It didn't need any more embellishments – the Blessed Mother already came out of it very well. Unfortunately, the nun went on to suggest that the reason the Virgin Mary had intervened was because this woman on the subway happened to also be a virgin and was saving herself for marriage.

If someone told me now what the nun told me then, I would be horrified. But at the time, I felt nothing but boredom and a vague desire for the talk to end. I had already decided at that point that the Church wasn't for me, and I had categorised this as another boring lecture from a guest speaker. When you're a teenager, you think you are already a fully formed adult. I didn't understand all of the impressions this nun was trying to make on us – about sexuality, about trying to moralise virginity, about who does and does not deserve to be a victim of sexual violence.

I like to think this incident was incredible enough to be etched in all of our memories forever. But when I ask my school friends about it now, a lot of them respond with blank stares – or worse, offer up even more bizarre anecdotes about our eccentric 'guest speakers', which I have no memory of. Una, a friend who was a couple of years ahead of me, told me about a time a woman came in and told us horoscopes were evil. And another speaker, who had been brought in to talk about something innocuously Catholic, veered into what was basically an oral retelling of *The Silent Scream*. A lot of us had tiny golden feet pinned to our upturned collars. I remember wearing one but didn't know what it meant: the 'precious feet' pin is a popular form of anti-abortion propaganda. The feet are the 'actual size and shape of a 10-week-old baby's feet'. I only realised this in my twenties, when a pair was anonymously posted to me while I was working at a newspaper and writing about abortion rights.

Those speakers could have told me anything and I would have believed it. We were operating in a complete vacuum of information. And the misinformation we spread about sex ourselves was astounding.

At the age of about 14 we started going to these teenage discos in the local sports centre. They were sponsored by Cidona, which still makes me laugh. We all went with naggins stuffed in our bras. For many of us, the bras were holding absolutely nothing else at the time so this was fine.

Your sartorial choices for these discos were restricted to a very regimented uniform: snow boots, a ra-ra skirt and some sort of heinous Lycra top. These came in pink, white or black: the colour combination was your choice.

By day we filed into the sports centre with our Jane Norman bags filled with tracksuits and clandestine tampons for our PE classes. But by night, for the discos, the centre turned into a dark cavern with crap green lighting and that Eurodance hard trance music that all Irish teenagers listened to for some reason.

Dark corners and bathroom cubicles were hives of misguided petting and sloppy shifting. One night a girl in our class had been sitting on a boy's lap while they were shifting, and it turned into a … climactic experience for him. To be crystal clear, they both still had all their clothes on. From his perspective, this must have been a humiliating experience. Sometimes I wonder how much time that boy spent worrying about that story getting out; imagining all of us cackling at our lockers the next day at the expense of his sexual inexperience. Unfortunately for him, the story did get out at the lockers the next day. But fortunately for him, our response was way too moronic to focus on the obvious. Everyone decided that our friend was now, unfortunately but certainly, pregnant. We thought semen had the same properties usually only seen in heat-seeking missiles, and that it could penetrate two sets of underwear, a good pair of jeans and a ra-ra skirt and head straight for the egg.

I was recently at a fancy grown-up dinner party with some of my friends from school who are now fancy grown-ups. Somehow we started talking about our sexual ignorance at school and remembered how a girl in our class used to terrorise us with all kinds of 'information'. This girl, who we'll call Sophie, had had sex long before any of the rest of us, and our long-term virginity made us the perfect vulnerable audience for her mad stories. Sophie blithely mentioned one day how, sometimes, boys could accidentally have sex with the 'wrong hole'. No, not that one. Sophie convinced us that boys could accidentally have sex with your urinary tract. We deduced that this must be where UTIs come from.

Between the talks from orthodox anti-sex Catholics and zealous nuns, and the proliferation of fake news from anarchists like Sophie, we really could have done with some formal sex education. No such luck.

We fiddled with bunsen burners in the science lab as Mr Collins, our biology teacher, dryly talked us through the absolute basics of a menstrual cycle and fertilisation with a sparse and clinical diagram. There was very little scintillating detail involved.

For reasons unknown, someone decided that the more practical rather than biological elements of sex education were squarely in the remit of religion class. Maybe they wanted to keep the two subjects together in a nod to the Madonna/whore dichotomy.

One teacher in my school was particularly scary. She was very petite, but her size was inversely proportional to the amount of terror she was able to wield over us. She had a set of dentures that seemed to be perpetually loose. That meant she would drag out words as she spoke, as if she was giving herself more time to try to scoop her teeth back into her mouth before she got to the last syllable. This slightly distorted the way she said 'girls', which is how everyone addressed us in the Ard Scoil. 'NGgggaaaaaahrls,' she would drawl, striking fear into our hearts.

Guess who was teaching us the day we got to the chapter on sex education in religion class? She asked us to open our books on the relevant page. We stared down at it, the word S-E-X emblazoned across it. It was a slow dawning. We realised what was about to happen. The tension built. She stared at us, unspeaking, unmoving, wearing her favourite expression (pure loathing). We all glanced at each other helplessly. The silence went on. It was excruciating. Finally, eventually, someone snapped. It was like the hiss of air from a pressurised container: a snigger. Only a second long, but more than enough.

'*Right!*' she yelled as she snapped the book closed. 'If you ngahrls can't be mature about it, we won't do it at all.'

And that was it. My sex education. It didn't occur to us to read that particular chapter ourselves, in our own time.

But there was a bigger, better part of the Ard Scoil that had a radically different understanding of Catholic education, which I am extremely grateful for. Having been within the warmth of an all-girls school, with a predominantly female staff, I understand that there is a lot to be said for it. In many ways, my Catholic school is probably the closest I'll ever get to a feminist utopia.

Many other parts of my life have involved places where there only seemed to be space for one promising young woman. I'm ashamed of the times when I saw another woman as a personal threat. At the Ard Scoil there was enough space for all of us. Girls who excelled and exceeded were not regarded with exception or qualification. In my school, a girl was the best at everything. Competition between us was healthy and nothing to do with gendered jealousy. Nobody's ambition was a threat to anybody else.

The bond between us was so strong that we were sentimental and nostalgic about it even while we were still in school. We talked all the time about how we'd never find another group like us once we left. A beautifully kind teacher called Mrs Dowdall bestowed us with a motto: *mol an óige, agus tiocfaidh sí* – praise the youth, and they will blossom. We took that to extremes with each other. Individual successes – in team sports, fleadh ceoils, debating competitions, academic tests, whatever – felt like a win for the whole year. We seized on annual talent shows, pantomimes and charity fashion shows as an opportunity to showcase and praise each other. Even during some truly dreadful performances, the room would be rippling with tension as everyone kept serious, respectful faces and then clapped earnestly when the person was finished.

My favourite was the school masses. Fr Flor, our school chaplain, gave us a huge amount of freedom. We got to decorate the Friary Church in Dungarvan and incorporate our own songs and poems and speeches. Nothing from the traditional mass ceremony was ever sacrificed – we just got to embellish it a bit. The result was totally joyous. If normal mass was like those ones, I probably would have been back long ago.

We were blessed with teachers who had wonderful interpretations of Catholic teaching. Bean de Paor was our very glamorous English teacher, who looked and still looks like Christine Baranski. She would often sneak us out of school for illicit walks during class to see in real life the beauty of the natural world that Yeats and Keats and Heaney were all writing about. I met her recently and she told me that she still has her own version of an illicit walk on Sunday mornings. When everyone else is going to mass in her town of Youghal, County Cork, she's going in the opposite direction down to the coast. 'That's worshipping God to me,' she told me.

We took social responsibility very seriously. We were zealous about charitable causes and fundraising for Amnesty International and Concern. The Christian ethos of the school seemed to be intertwined with social justice in a way that made feminism and Catholicism synonymous. For a long time as an adult, I thought that Catholicism and feminism were two mutually exclusive things, rather than being so complementary that I actually think I am only one because of the other.

The Ard Scoil certainly never saw promoting women's rights as something beyond its remit as a Catholic school. Thanks to the initiative of a former principal called Angela Conway, International Women's Day became one of the major events in the school calendar. This was 15 or even 20 years ago – way before International Women's Day became an exercise in virtuous branding for rich companies. When I was in school, teachers used it as an opportunity to try to overwhelm us with inspiration. We would file into the senior hall and sit and listen as a range of brilliant women spoke to us. Some of the speakers took a year to arrange. One of the Marys was there one year – McAleese or Robinson, I'm not sure which. Former students who had gone on to become teachers, scientists or nurses were often invited back too. What I liked about the Ard Scoil's version of International Women's Day was that it didn't just rely on powerful, rich and famous women. A former president could speak on the same day as a former student who was now a primary school teacher. They made an effort to appeal to everyone's aspirations. So sometimes, when it was a topic I had no interest in, I would zone out completely. Then one day, they invited in a journalist called Justine McCarthy.

Chapter 4

Justine McCarthy is one of the best journalists and commentators in Ireland, and exactly the kind of person my school had the good sense to spot as a galvanising force for lethargic teenage girls. I remember almost exactly where I was sitting for the talk. She stood out because she spoke to us as if we were adults. She was standing on stage with a glamorous mess of tight blonde curls that would shake in punctuation as she put the world to rights. The way Justine talks in real life is exactly like her columns: precise and polished and powerful. There isn't a word wasted.

I immediately decided that whatever this woman did for a job I would like to do as well. I was too shy to ask a question at the end in front of everyone, so I slunk up to her afterwards. She gave me her email address. Years later, when I was in the middle of my journalism degree in Cardiff, I wrote to her at her new job in the *Sunday Times* and asked if she remembered me. She helped put me in touch with the editor, whom I successfully pleaded with for a work-experience placement. I finished my week there with a front-page story about how some pharmacies were ripping women off for the morning-after pill. In 2015, when the *Sunday Times* set up a sister daily paper – *The Times*, Ireland edition – I left my full-time job at BBC Wales and moved to Dublin just to get two shifts a week at the new paper. I think that Richie Oakley, the editor, wasn't expecting much from me. He suggested I could try waitressing on the side to earn enough to live on. But it quickly turned into a full-time job. And I got to work in the same office as Justine.

I was 24 and had moved into a flat in Dublin with Mary, my friend from school. We used to savour Justine's weekly columns for the *Sunday Times*.

Justine wrote about the Church through the height of the sex abuse scandals. She told me that she was on a plane to New York to interview Annie Murphy the day the Eamon Casey story broke. 'That day, on that flight, I thought: my God, this is the beginning of the end,' she said. 'Sure, that was in the ha'penny place compared to everything else.' I read all her columns about the Magdalene laundries, the National Maternity Hospital scandal and the 2018 papal visit, which were all excoriating.

Criticising the Church comes easily to a lot of people: it takes little skill to collate a list of its failings. And many people take great joy and satisfaction in doing so. But when I read Justine's columns, they feel more like the words of a righteous Christian. In 2018 she wrote about the materialism of the World Meeting of Families in Dublin: 'Can Catholics whose souls are not discomfited by this monetised idolatry credibly call themselves followers of the Christ who flew into a fury and flung the money-lenders from the temple?' She has a decent moral compass, which was what I needed.

I wanted to go back to the Church, but I wasn't sure if it was the right thing to do. If the Catholic Church wasn't guilty of devastating and sometimes fatal misogyny in Ireland, it was – at best – an accessory to the crime. The Irish State's first century is pockmarked by the barbarity of Magdalene laundries and mother-and-baby homes. Ireland was hardly the only country with backwards attitudes to women in the first half of the twentieth century. But here, female sexuality was a sin as well as a social ill. So we got the Church to manage these fallen women, with devastating consequences. Priests were afforded the kind of authority over women's reproductive rights that one would rarely see awarded to even the best gynaecologist. The tyranny of this unholy union between a sexist Church and a backwards State, and the culture it created, was still at the height of its powers in 1980s Ireland, as seen with the Kerry Babies case, for example.

But a good Catholic would forgive and forget, especially as the modern Irish Catholic Church has conceded that it made mistakes in the past. However, while you can't directly compare incarceration in a laundry with banning women priests, it is true to say that the policies and views of the Catholic Church remain sexist today.

The more I learn, the more certain I feel that the place in a church for a woman is down on her hands and knees, in a pair of rubber gloves, cleaning the floor of the altar. You can arrange the flowers; you can make the tea for the priest. Sure, you can hand out communion or do a reading. You can't be a deacon. Do not dream of the priesthood.

I assumed, when I started trying to find a way back to the Church, that I'd be disappointed by how robust the argument against women priests would be. I was imagining some sort of profound scripture, which had thus far eluded me, that would explain clearly and unambiguously that God was definitely all for a sexist two-tier Church. Was I in for a treat or what.

I knew that all of the apostles were men, and this was often cited in the argument against ordaining women, but I never in my wildest dreams thought that that was it. That's the whole argument? Most of the apostles were fishermen as well, but the Vatican has not yet decreed that there should be a dedicated quota of priests who've earned a living on a boat. (One of the apostles was also an embezzler, but in fairness to the Irish Catholic Church, they did manage to tick that box with a couple of priests.)

Smarter people than me have, of course, flagged their concerns with a major international institution basing their HR and equal-opportunities policy on societal norms from AD 33. But this is where the Vatican really came into its own. The Vatican argued that to suggest that Jesus only chose men because he existed within a society that was sexist would be wrong because Jesus would have been above sexism. So, as I see it, the Vatican basically concedes that excluding women on the basis of sex would be wrong by suggesting that that is exactly the kind of social norm that Jesus would have overridden. Yet, in his name, the Church perpetuates the same kinds of sexism. The way I read it, a doctrine from 1976 ('Declaration on the Question of the Admission of Women to the Ministerial Priesthood') clarifies that Jesus would of course have been able to do what 266 popes have never managed and treat women equally. He just chose not to, so that must mean women are unfit to be priests. It's so kitten-weak I'd almost prefer if they gave their own balls-out, bare-faced misogyny as a reason instead.

So I had major trouble with the concept of going back to the Church, in case it meant giving my tacit approval to an organisation that was so exasperatingly crap at veiling its sexism. It also felt selfish to put my own desire for religion above the terrible things that the Church did to other women. On the other hand, the Church was starting to appeal to me now because I was starting to see Catholicism and feminism as complementary. I had to find out if it was possible to support a version of Catholicism that agitates for equality for everyone – including women – without endorsing the sexist institution of the Church.

That's when I turned to Justine for help. She met me in the café above the Kilkenny Shop, on Nassau Street in

Dublin. I love that place because every table you eavesdrop on feels like a scene snatched from a Maeve Binchy novel. People butter scones and pour tea and gossip in the way you only do when it's a long overdue catch-up. It could be 1999, 2009 or 2019 in there; there's little to discern which decade it is, in the best way.

I've mentioned how Justine had reported on the Church at its worst; she'd seen the true horror of what it did up close. The entire time, her faith had weathered the storm. But in the end, she couldn't stay.

'I had three good priests in my life,' she told me, over coffee and pancakes.

The first was her brother-in-law, Martin, who she said was 'the most normal, fun-loving person you could meet'. Another was a grand-uncle, Chris, who had worked in Australia as a priest. When Justine was covering the abuse scandal in the Church for the *Irish Independent* in the 1990s, he would send her a little letter from his home in Cork every so often saying, 'Keep going, the Church needs to hear this, keep going.' The third was Fr Seán Fagan. Fr Fagan was censured by the Catholic Church after he questioned the Church's teaching on sexual morality.

'Seán Fagan was treated absolutely appallingly,' Justine said. 'He was a theologian. The Church bought up all his books and banned him from contributing to newspapers or broadcast media. He couldn't even write a letter to the *Irish Times* anymore. They put him under a vow of public silence.'

Fr Fagan had also been banned from telling anyone about the Vatican's censorship.

'It was like a super-injunction,' Justine said. 'It destroyed his life. This good man, he was so hurt by it.'

Fr Fagan passed away in 2016. After all three of her 'good priests' had died, Justine felt like she couldn't stay, especially when she saw how women were written out of the liturgy by the Church.

'I really regret that I found that I, finally, couldn't stay,' Justine said. 'I cannot come to terms with the misogyny of the Catholic Church. It is the most misogynistic institution that I have ever experienced … This is my spiritual and cultural heritage, and nothing has ever made me feel so unwanted in my life.'

I'm worried about that, too. It's bad enough to feel your Church thinks you are lesser because you're a woman. It's worse to feel they think you're a pariah.

Justine said she received letters from people abusing her for trying to destroy the Church. 'That was the last thing I wanted to do! I wanted to help it,' she said.

The letters are a regular feature. The week before she spoke to me, she'd written a column on the lack of women in the Dáil. The letters she'd received that week were '100 per cent from men'.

'Telling me my hormones were all over the place, I was having a hissy fit, I need to calm down. I'm a man-hater. I'd be better off in the North Korean government. My opinion was nonsense. That I'm stupid. That they're taking out their rosary beads and praying for Ireland to be protected from people like me. They call themselves Christians? That's just blind ignorance,' she said.

The ways that the 'good Catholics' of Ireland have come out against Justine are jaw-dropping.

'The former Bishop of Ferns threatened to rape me. In 1994, when I was five months pregnant,' Justine told me. 'I didn't write about it [for the paper] until the report on Ferns came out ... It was the splash in the Indo on a Saturday, and I was told that at a church in Drumcondra the next morning, a priest had denounced me from the altar. That's Catholicism in his mind? I was the victim of a serious crime by a senior member of the Catholic Church, and I was the one who was in the wrong?'

Who could blame her for leaving? I regret that she did, because I think she's one of the most Christian people I know, but I don't know if my faith would survive that kind of treatment. Hers did for a long time, but eventually it became too much.

In the end, her advice to me was to return and try to stay, too. 'They wouldn't greet you with open arms, and I think it would be hard, but I think it probably would be for the greater good. You have to have the critical voices inside there,' she said. 'When everyone who has a criticism to make leaves, that's when the Church is in its greatest peril.'

I know this is the answer that I want because I've been

honest with myself about how much I want my faith back. But I need to make sure it's not the easy answer to take.

Supporting the Church is something I can do if I know there's even the faintest, tiniest, most miniscule hope or chance of reform. That crowd are big into miracles, after all. But if its attitude to women is rotten to the core, then maybe I can't.

———— ⚜ ————

The Jesus I think of is the one who sat with the woman at the well and who had a deep relationship with Mary Magdalene. (In the spirit of candour, sometimes when I imagine these Biblical stories in my mind, the role of Jesus is being played by Hozier.) For help, I turn to the Bible.

The Bible doesn't have an index, which I think is a missed opportunity. They should design one that makes it searchable by crisis. For example: heartbreak? Please see Psalm 43:18. Are you about to cheat on your partner? Please see Proverbs 6:32.

I want to find something to help me understand if I'm right to be questioning the Church's attitudes to women, or if picking and choosing policies makes me a plastic Catholic, I try flicking through the New Testament at random and see where my finger lands.

I get John 14:23: 'Jesus replied, "Anyone who loves me will obey my teaching."' OK, that sounds bad for me. However, maybe the Church's interpretation of the teaching on women is wrong? Maybe this is him coming down on my side? Who knows? This is way too subjective. It reminds me of the time I tried to teach myself how to read tarot cards. Sure, you can see anything you want in them.

Instead, I turn to the internet. I find an article called '20 uplifting Bible verses for women'. Perfect. I have a little scroll.

It does not start well. The first few are from Proverbs, where someone seems to have been flat-out bitching about their wife.

'Better to live on a corner of the roof than share a house with a quarrelsome wife' and 'Better to live in a desert than with a quarrelsome and nagging wife.' Then: 'Wives, submit yourselves to your own husbands as you do to the Lord.'

This is followed by some choice words from Timothy, who sounds like quite the character: 'I also want the women to dress modestly ... A woman should learn in quietness and full submission ... I do not permit a woman to teach or to assume authority over a man; she must be quiet ... But women will be saved through childbearing – if they continue in faith, love and holiness with propriety.'

I scroll back to the top of the page, incredulous. Yes, it still said 'uplifting' Bible verses about women. Uplifting for who? If I saw this on Reddit, I'd think I'd stumbled upon an incel's manifesto. I feel worse than ever. Seeking IRL counsel, I go to see a priest.

When Fr Joe McDonald arrived to meet me in a café in Celbridge, I was one of the only customers there, but he still walked straight past me. I looked around in confusion. It was just me at a table on my own, and two other men sharing a table across the room. I caught his attention and smiled, and he came over looking apologetic.

'I assumed, because of the subject matter, that you'd be a lot older,' he said, with the cadence of someone who grew up in Belfast.

A man came over to take our order and asked, in mock outrage, how Fr McDonald was managing to have coffee with 'a nice young woman'. It was obvious that he was quite a popular priest, and very gregarious. (As soon as we started chatting, he joked that he couldn't abandon the priesthood and the celibacy that goes with it now, because he wouldn't be accepted onto the next season of *Love Island*.) He ordered a full Irish and I asked for a scone.

A friend had told me about Fr McDonald. She was local and had been to his Christmas mass, where he apologised to the congregation for the wrongs of the Catholic Church. He has a reformer's agenda, and he's spoken to the media frequently about his objections to some of the Church's teaching.

In 2017 he did an interview on the *Late Late Show* where he spoke about why the Catholic Church should change its approach to LGBT+ people. Fr McDonald also used the same interview to talk about how he had been sexually abused by a priest growing up in West Belfast.

While affable, when he talked about his love of Jesus Christ he was always profound. There are layers to his vocation, which he compared to a marriage: a deep and lasting relationship that you put work into to reap the rewards. 'The thing that brings you in is not what will keep you,' he said.

As we chatted, he wasn't long setting me straight on the worries I had about how the Catholic Church views women.

'Jesus's relationship with women: we have edited out a lot of that. You have to remember that everything you get about Jesus is presented to you through a male, clerical filter,' he said.

I told him about my luckless attempt to get help from the Bible, which he seemed to think was a bad idea. Fr McDonald told me that there wasn't a whole lot of *meas* for reading the Bible in Catholicism. In fact, when he was growing up in Belfast it was actively discouraged. 'I remember people saying the Bible is for Protestants and Catholics go to mass. We were told the Bible was dangerous.' Instead, the Bibles would remain pristine and unread, in huge frames hanging on the wall.

'People have no concept of the impact of women in the Bible. Absolutely none. And sometimes the impact they had was very significant.'

I write down some names that he gives me: Naomi, Ruth, Esther and, of course, Bridget. Fr McDonald goes on to explain that he doesn't think the faith is misogynistic, but he certainly thinks that the Church is.

'If I use the word "misogyny" publicly, I'll get a priest who'll come after me and say it's too strong a word and it means hatred of women. And I say, yeah, it's not that we hate women, we just want you to keep quiet,' he told me. 'It's: I'd be happy if you'd arrange the flowers there on the altar, and would you bake me an apple tart? But don't be thinking you'll be coming up here beside me to talk about your faith.'

One day, before the referendum on the Eighth Amendment, he met a woman who was working in Maynooth. She was a 'dedicated member of the Church'. She told Fr McDonald how the Irish Catholic bishops had been having a meeting upstairs in one of the buildings about their pro-life policy ahead of the vote. All these male clerics, many of them elderly, were talking about the ethics of life in utero. And underneath them, in the basement, where the secretarial work was being done, were about twelve women of childbearing age. None of them thought to consult or involve any of their female underlings. Fr McDonald said it was the perfect metaphor for the Church.

'They'd no trouble talking about premature births, miscarriages, longing for a baby and not getting there. Their voice was so limited and narrow without the feminine, and the feminine of that age in particular,' he said.

We talked for a long time over sausages and scones, and he started to tell me about another worry he had. As people like me were driven away from the Church – Fr McDonald called it a 'haemorrhage' – he said it created an opportunity for 'restorationists'.

'These are people who want to restore us to the "great days" of the 1950s,' Fr McDonald said sarcastically. 'Sometimes the people who are drawn to the Church at a time like this, when there is a big gap, can be very extreme.'

And what did he think about what happened in the 1950s? Fr McDonald leaned back in his chair and breathed out. He sounded almost incredulous. 'I marvel at how we managed in the 1950s to preach a message of fear, shame, guilt when in fact the message is love, joy, freedom. And we did it in Technicolor, in Dolby Stereo. We didn't whisper it. We did it with a roar,' he said.

I mentioned in passing that I'd spoken to some other priests who agree with him.

'Anonymously?' he said.

'Yes …' I said, and this seemed to frustrate him.

'It's so difficult: even the guys who are interested in reform don't have any hope for it. They don't see a way of voicing or channelling it,' he said.

Huge sweeping reform will not happen anytime soon – that is obvious to Fr McDonald and to me. He explained how he's trying to work with what he has. Archbishop Diarmuid Martin had just given him permission to sell two 'big houses' that the parish owns.

'I live in a big house, which is probably the Celbridge equivalent of Downton Abbey. It's a huge house, it's an old house, it's a privilege to live in it but, I mean, how do I get up on a Sunday and preach on Jesus of Nazareth and home-lessness while I live in a mansion?' he said.

He was moving into an old convent and planned to recruit four or five lay people to help him run the parish in a more democratic and collective way. He told me that the leader of this group would 'hopefully' be a woman. It's called the Roncalli Community, after Pope John XXIII – Angelo Roncalli. 'A hero of mine,' Fr McDonald said about the reformer pope. 'If it works, it would be a happier priesthood and a more fulfilled laity,' he said.

This was small, but it was what I was looking for: hope of reform.

I told him about the worries I still had: about my presence in the Church giving my 'tacit' approval to the bad stuff. He couldn't disagree with me more. 'If you said to me: "I'm going to resolve a lot of these difficulties and I'm going to stay and accept the Church as it is," I'd be saying, no, don't do that. I'd be disappointed. And I don't think it would be good for you long term,' Fr McDonald told me. 'But if you said to me: "I believe there is something there. I believe a lot of stuff should be dumped in terms of attitudes, and lack of mercy and harshness and all that, I'm not going to buy into that stuff ..." At least consider staying, but stay in order to be part of the reform. Don't let the bastards write you out.'

I'd thought about staying to spite the institutional Church, but I hadn't thought about staying *in spite of* the Church. I suppose if women waited for formal invitations before we joined institutions we wanted to change, we'd be nowhere. And if we refused to engage with institutions that were riddled with sexism, we would have opted out of society completely a long time ago. When I was getting the bus home from Kildare, one thing that Fr McDonald said stuck in my head more than anything else. 'Don't let the bastards write you out' sounded as good as Gospel to me.

Chapter 5

There was one incentive that could get my lazy teen-age arse out of bed early for school, and that was gossip. After nuking any natural shape out of my hair with every single degree of heat I could get out of a GHD, and the tactless application of a homogenous mask of foundation, I would be keen to get going by 8.15 a.m. I'd harass my younger sister into my car, zoom into school, park illegally and rush to the top floor of the senior building to the Sixth Year classrooms.

Each morning of our Leaving Certificate year, we would mill between bathrooms and lockers before gathering at the back of a classroom for an intense chat. This was an appointment attendance, like a daily White House brief-ing, but just for our little universes. We would lean against tables, which were still stacked on top of each other from our sweet release at 4 p.m. the day before. The tables would be laid out again for class when the bell rang at 9 a.m., and not a moment sooner. The actual act of learning felt like a persistent nuisance that we all patiently put up with. That half an hour of chat before 9 a.m. was the most treasured part of the morning. We would then endure two hours of class before rushing to talk to each other again, at 11 a.m.

Often we were picking up chats that had ended only a few hours before on Bebo or on the phone. This was fine – conversation material was a renewable resource. People marvel at sports pundits who manage to get an hour of televised analysis out of a very dull game. But teenage girls do this for years at a time, no problem. The twists and turns of our little lives were so interesting to us that we would analyse them for hours on end. How we felt about exams, boys and parents were all topics of crucial import.

We felt we were the centre of the universe. For example, one January a local radio station invited a fortune teller to make predictions for the coming year. This fortune teller predicted, with staggering confidence, that there would be a shooting in one of the local schools. This prediction might sound unbelievable, and also like grossly irresponsible broadcasting, but when we heard it, it was not a matter of if it would happen but when. Because if something was happening anywhere in the world, why wouldn't it happen to us?

We loved conversation. If we'd temporarily exhausted all the material from our social lives, we would find ways to talk about other things. Sometimes, we talked about television.

One bright morning we were gathered at the back of a classroom for a chat, as usual. We had stuffed ourselves into a corner next to a coat rack, where blue O'Neills school hoodies hung next to coats with fur-trimmed hoods. Some of us leaned against the coats or snuggled into them. Four or five plastic chairs were stacked in piles next to me, and some of the girls were awkwardly trying to perch on them. We were talking about *Grey's Anatomy*.

An exciting episode of *Grey's Anatomy* or *Desperate Housewives* would be an agenda-setting item the next morning in school. It makes me feel like the oldest woman on earth to talk about television 'in my day' being run on a set, immovable schedule of one episode a week around which we would dutifully organise the rest of our evenings.

Even girls like me, who didn't watch *Grey's Anatomy*, would be included in the discussion. Normally, the discussion was fawning. But on this day, it was outraged. There had been a gay kiss between two characters in *Grey's Anatomy* and in 2008 this was still the source of some fuss and controversy.

'I just think it's disgusting,' one friend said and asked what would have happened had her younger brother seen it. Another girl added that it didn't have to be so 'in your face'. A few of us stayed pretty quiet and didn't say much at all. I didn't really see the harm in a same-sex kiss, and eventually mumbled my dissent in some half-hearted way.

One of the girls turned on me instantly.

'Well, is there something you need to tell us, Ellen?'

Then the bell went, and we dispersed. I stayed still. I felt my face get hot, and I swallowed hard. I was very embarrassed. The suggestion was clear: my defence of two fictional, handsome doctors was incontrovertible evidence that I was a secret lesbian. And I was mortified. Not because I was gay, but because I was straight. I was as much a fan of signing an Amnesty International petition as your next self-righteous convent-school girl, but I was definitely not a proud LGBT+ ally. Finding out I was gay was up there on my list of teenage fears with discovering thrush and revealing my real age to local nightclub bouncers. There was no debate: not being straight was an oddity and an embarrassment. Of all the LGBT+ people I know now from my hometown, I can only remember one who came out before they left school. Most other people only did it in the safety of college.

The word 'homophobic' is a big one, and it causes a big reaction. People associate homophobia with teeth-gnashing, backwards loons who wish nothing less than death on gay people. Most real-life homophobia is very different to that. When you call someone who is otherwise nice and reasonable 'homophobic', it makes them balk. Sometimes, it can entrench their views and radicalise them against 'political correctness'. No, homophobia couldn't mean people like them.

I know it would hurt my friend's' feelings to hear it, but there is no doubt in my mind that we held very homophobic views when we were in school. And it was harmful. It came from a place of ignorance, rather than malice – like most prejudices do. Ard Scoil na nDeise, our school, is a Ceist school. Ceist stands for 'Catholic Education an Irish Schools'

Trust', and it represents over a hundred Catholic secondary schools in Ireland. At school, from what I remember, we were taught absolutely nothing about the existence of gay people, which is perfectly in line with the Irish Catholic Church's education policy. The Church has a 16-page document called 'Guidelines on Relationships and Sexuality Education' that does not mention same-sex relationships or LGBT+ people once. As far as the Church's education policy is concerned, gay people may as well be a myth.

In an atmosphere like that, it is no wonder so many people didn't come out. So not only did we not know much about gay people, we also thought we didn't know many gay people. I am conscious of the perils of remembering this solely through the perspective of a privileged straight person, so I double-checked my version of events with a friend who has come out in the years since we left the Ard Scoil. She agreed that a lot of us said some pretty homophobic stuff in school, including her. In her words, 'Jaysus, I was an awful c***.' 'I dont think the Ard Scoil was outwardly homophobic, but the absence of gay education is as good as,' she said. She had even described a teacher she didn't like as a lesbian for about four years.

I always kept a vigilant eye on my ever-changing and new teenage feelings in case I was gay. Any fleeting crushes I may have had on girls – which was hardly a unique experience – would send me fleeing to the advice pages of teenage girls' magazines. I wanted to know the same thing that almost every anxious teenager wants to know: am I normal? And from what I understood, gay was not normal. The magazines would often seek to reassure you that having a crush on a girl did not automatically mean you were gay, rather than explaining that it would have been fine if you were. Our fear and misunderstanding of gay people ranged from the bleak to the batshit. Anyone who was in any way different or strange was branded gay. It was an umbrella term for weird girls.

We were definitely prejudiced against gay people. But in fewer than six years' time, we would all be voting Yes in the marriage equality referendum. We would be putting 'YES FOR EQUALITY' and 'LOVE WINS' stickers on our social media profiles, as was standard for most people our age. What had happened in the interim was that we had left school, moved on in life and learned a little bit.

I had also left the Church. Maybe 'left' is too strong an adjective; it implies thought and action. I think like most people my age, it was a slow drift. In my late teens, I couldn't see a universe where this archaic and backward institution would have any place or relevance in my life. I was confident about this to the point of arrogance. To me, it was black and white: the Church presided over some really awful things; therefore, it was an awful institution. I started whingeing about being brought to Mass on hungover Sunday mornings until it was eventually too much hassle for my mam to bother with. I was fond of the Mass we had in school, but I think I saw that as a sentimental quirk of the Ard Scoil. Before I knew it, I was only darkening the door of a church for Christmas and the occasional funeral. By the time I moved to Cardiff to go to college, I hadn't realised it, but it had been years since I had left the faith. It wasn't until I was passing a church on a walk to lectures one day that I realised what had happened: I wasn't part of organised religion, and hadn't been for years. I hadn't even missed it.

I didn't meet out and proud LGBT+ people until I was in college. My house of six straight girls and one gay guy would spend an inordinate amount of time in Cardiff's gay bars, which were called things like WOW and Pulse. It was a fair exchange: our housemate got to go on the pull, and we had a brief respite from the routine generic sexual harassment that was guaranteed in all the other university bars. That, and the music was better.

I don't remember consciously deciding to cop on and sort out my weird views about LGBT+ people. I credit my views changing to finally existing in a world where being gay was normal. If 13 years of Catholic education didn't manage to indoctrinate me as a homophobe, I doubt a liberal gay globalist conspiracy would have been able to indoctrinate me the other way in the first few months of college. Being not weird about gay people just seemed like … the most normal way to behave. I was embarrassed by how I used to think.

So, a happy ending: the straight girl is finally enlightened. Broader societal changes had been more potent and influential than the vacuum of information in which I had previously existed. But that's not really the issue for me.

Even now, Ceist schools like my former one still follow the Catholic Church's teaching on homosexuality. In the decade since I was in school, societal views about LGBT+ issues have changed radically in Ireland but the Church's have not. The Irish government has been promising to reform sex education since the referendum on the Eighth Amendment, but recently admitted that it doesn't have the right to force Catholic schools to change their teaching.

Some Catholic schools still farm out their relationship and sexuality education to external groups, like the people who came in and bamboozled me with that roll of Sellotape. Again, these groups refuse to acknowledge the existence of LGBT+ people, same-sex relationships or contraception.

A group called Lifeworks goes into schools across Ireland to talk to students about relationship and sexuality education all the time. It is anti-abortion and excludes any mention of same-sex relationships from its talks. It regularly visits Ceist schools. Ceist told me that 'Ceist endorses Lifeworks but invitations are a matter for each individual school.' Two of the directors of Lifeworks, Emma Sisk and Katie Murray, are activists with the Pro Life Campaign. Lifeworks is listed at the same business address as the Pro Life Campaign. The registered address of Lifeworks is the same as that of an engineering firm run by Sean Ascough, who sits on the board of the Iona Institute. The Iona Institute said that Lifeworks 'is not connected' to it. (The more time I spend reading about conservative Catholic activists in Ireland, the smaller and smaller the pool of them seems to get.)

If my parents had wanted to send me to a secondary school that was not Catholic, there were no options in our town. That's the case in a lot of towns in Ireland. So small arch-conservative groups, who have devoted themselves to homophobic and anti-abortion causes, get to come in and teach Irish teenagers about sex and relationships just because those teenagers go to a Catholic school. Children are being taught material that could lead to homophobia and discrimination in the name of Catholicism. That's before you even consider the damage these talks could do to teenagers who are LGBT+ and also immersed in an environment where homophobia can flourish. Again, all done in the name of God.

Conservative Catholics, faced with calls for more diversity in schools, have rallied for what they describe as the right of their schools to be 'truly Catholic'.

What does that mean? From what I can gather, it means schools where you can teach children and teenagers that they should only have sex with people of the opposite sex; abortion is evil; contraception is wrong; and anyway, you should be saving sex until after you're married. Putting the moral arguments aside for a moment, does that not sound kind of weird? Once again, I feel confronted by a version of Catholicism that portrays the faith as a strange club for people who are obsessed with other people's sex lives.

I don't buy that all parents give their tacit support to that sort of right-wing propaganda just by virtue of choosing a Catholic school for their children. Even if you exclude parents whose children attend Catholic schools only because there are no other options, we know by now that in Ireland a lot of Catholics are in favour of LGBT+ equality. I've seen no evidence to suggest that the Venn diagram of Catholics and No voters in 2015 is a perfect circle. And, like me, the majority of Yes voters were probably brought up with a Catholic education – before roundly rejecting its teachings on LGBT+ people. So where does that leave us?

A study by BeLonG To in 2018 found that 90 per cent of young Irish LGBT+ people struggle with their mental health. With its enduring influence over sex education, the Catholic Church has to be doing serious and potentially lethal damage. I find it impossible to believe that it isn't. And what could possibly justify doing that in the name of Catholicism?

———— ♧ ————

I try to find out for myself what the Bible says about same-sex relationships. Initially, I thought this would be a swift task, as the Bible would presumably be so unequivocal about it. Unfortunately, it's more confusing than I thought. I decide to start with Sodom and Gomorrah, a Bible story I associate almost exclusively with the language of raving homophobes lashing out at Ireland's apparent cursed journey towards wife-swapping sodomy. The Book of Genesis talks about the city of Sodom where Lot, a nephew of Abraham, was visited by two beautiful male angels. A mob of men surrounded the house and demanded that Lot bring the angels out 'that we may know them carnally'. This means rape. Lot offered up his own two virgin daughters to the men, but they refused. It's a horrific story. The angels blinded the men who were trying to break down the door and then told Lot they were going to destroy Sodom because it was so sinful. This is how the term 'sodomite' became a derogatory term for gay people.

The story is popular among homophobes who like to sombrely talk about how the Bible clearly portrays sodomites as sick and perverse – as though the decision to be prejudicial against LGBT+ people is out of their hands. Once again, I am no theologian, but sexual violence is obviously a world away from consensual, loving, same-sex relationships. Would I have ever left the Church in the first place if it had managed to take the clear and obvious moral from this story about the sin of sexual violence as seriously as the perceived sin of same-sex relationships?

To compare appalling sexual violence to a normal relationship between two men seems disgusting to me. Many Christian groups that are sympathetic to LGBT+ campaigners have made the point that the way the Bible describes the relationship between King David and Prince Jonathan could be interpreted as a same-sex relationship. The Bible doesn't explicitly state what the nature of their relationship was, but it sounds intense and fairly homoerotic. They loved each other as they loved their own souls, and their souls were described as being knitted together. Those against the theory point out that a lot of friendships between heterosexual men in the Bible were described in ways that would seem intense to us today. Once again, I'm frustrated by the lack of clarity from the Bible and conscious of how easy it could be for the institutional Church to use it to support whatever position it likes. Though I do enjoy the idea of people trying to pass King David and Prince Jonathan off as just great pals altogether in the same way tabloids in the early 2000s would talk about two women who were clearly lesbians. Just two very, very, very close friends!

If I was a good Christian who was conscious of the damage of homophobia, I would be hoping for something a lot more robust and unequivocal from the Bible before going along with the Church's position on LGBT+ people. I look for more relevant passages from the Old Testament: 'You shall not lie with a male as with a woman; it is an abomination' and 'If a man lies with a male as with a woman, both of them have committed an abomination; they shall surely be put to death; their blood is upon them.'

Both of these passages are from Leviticus, a book which is infamously full of such mad rules that a lot of Christians disregard it. It's often cited by people who want to dismiss or criticise the Bible by pointing out how Leviticus forbade wearing clothes with mixed fabrics or sitting in the same spot as a woman who has her period. I would also be nervous about relying on these passages when looking for evidence that God hates gay people.

So, onto the New Testament. Paul talks a lot about same-sex relationships but I'm frustrated to find that this is also interpreted by some as being open to debate. When Paul describes same-sex relationships as 'unnatural', some argue that he means heterosexual people who have same-sex relationships. Others say that Paul's condemnation of same-sex activity is ambiguous, but others have claimed he's criticising lust.

Paul, for the record, also describes men with long hair as being unnatural – which is understood to reflect the social norms at the time. If Paul had his way, the Jesus that Irish Catholics are familiar with would be devoid of his glossy locks; as would Hozier.

Truth be told, I'm starting to get a little pissed off with the Bible now. There's so much room for interpretation, between translations of the texts and considerations of social norms of the time, that it appears both sides can find a way to decipher scripture in a way that suits them. There are really beautiful parts of the Bible that offer quite clear and accessible guidance on how to live as a good Christian, but when it comes to the things I really need help with, the Bible leaves me feeling at sea. Without being a theological scholar, I feel ill-equipped to read and interpret the relevant passages.

For me, it comes down to one core point. The negative consequences of certain interpretations of the Bible's teachings on the lives of gay people are clearly the antithesis of the way Jesus taught us to treat each other. And what Jesus said about kindness in the Bible is not open to interpretation. It doesn't ring true to me that God would want LGBT+ people to be ostracised and maligned and hurt in his name. Once again, I decide to ask someone else for help.

Chapter 6

To advise schools to teach about sexuality in a way that could contribute to homophobia is an egregious mistake by the Catholic Church. I had briefly written about this issue before, and any time I had Justin McAleese had been really helpful. Justin is an LGBT+ rights advocate and also a Catholic. People may also know him as Mary McAleese's son.

I wrote to him explaining my conflict and asked for help. Justin knows a lot about the Church and is also pretty critical of it. He made some time to answer my questions on the phone and was extremely friendly and patient. Speaking to him, I realised the sheer scale of the influence of the Church's guidance for schools.

'If you managed to change the Church's teaching on women or gay people, the impact it would have around the world would be phenomenal,' Justin told me. 'There are about half a billion Catholics; there are around 200 million children in school today in Catholic-provided education.

Think of the impact that a change in thinking would have on women and children who are trying to come to terms with their sexuality.'

Can you imagine? It would probably be one of the greatest social goods that the Church could do, almost overnight. It's almost trite to point out how education is the easiest way to eliminate prejudice. I think about the 2015 marriage equality referendum, and the older Catholics who spoke about voting Yes based on the gay people they had come to know. If you created a school environment where it was OK to come out, then those children would have come to the same conclusion it had taken me until my twenties to come to. You would be taking a major step towards eradicating homophobic abuse of young people at one of the most formative and at-risk stages of their lives in terms of their mental health.

'People can't say "it's nothing to do with me" – it is if your children are going to a Catholic school. Under the ethos and guidelines of that school, there is no mention of anything that isn't straight. So we all have a vested interest,' Justin said.

Ahead of the marriage equality referendum in 2015, while campaigning unsuccessfully for a No vote, Archbishop Eamon Martin had asked, 'What will we be expected to teach children in school about marriage or about homosexual acts?'

'Well,' Justin said, 'my question is: what are you currently teaching about them? But again, the Church is uncomfortable answering those questions.'

I spoke to Justin the day after the Pope had sent a tweet that Justin was concerned could have been perceived to be about Cardinal Pell. George Pell, the Australian cardinal, was at the centre of one of the most high-profile child sex abuse allegations in the Catholic Church. He was convicted in 2018 but released from prison a year later after his conviction was quashed. Pell emerged as a bit of a cause célèbre among conservative Catholics, who appeared to be suggesting that there was an element of a witch-hunt against clerics.

Hours after Pell left jail, the Pope tweeted: 'In these days of #Lent, we've been witnessing the persecution that Jesus underwent and how He was judged ferociously, even though He was innocent. Let us #PrayTogether today for all those persons who suffer due to an unjust sentence because someone had it in for them.'

The Pope didn't reference Pell directly, but it raised a lot of eyebrows. 'He didn't literally compare Pell to the persecution of Jesus ...' Justin laughed. 'But ...'

He's right, it is possible that the Pope was referencing Pell and quite a few people had read it in that way. Justin sounded both incredulous at this prospect, but also not one bit surprised. He is a devout Catholic, but he told me he's decided to leave the Church.

'I am just over the institutional Church, I don't think I could ever go back,' he said.

Justin has spent a lot of time in Rome over the last few years. His mother had been living there and he worked for

Ryanair so, sometimes, he would get free flights. 'Well,' he said, 'as much as anything is free with Ryanair.'

'I would have known a lot of liberal priests, but then what you discover ... I have come to the conclusion that those liberal priests are actually just as bad as the right-wing priests. Basically, they're just living a double life,' Justin said. 'They tell you what you want to hear, they talk the talk. But actually, they're part of the institution which, at the end of the day, tells them to do one thing and they're doing the other.'

I bristle a little when I hear this. Would that be me if I went back? I am far from the Vatican establishment, for sure, and I'm sure that those 'liberal priests' benefit more tangibly from the system of the institutional Church than I would. But spiritually, wouldn't I be just as bad to turn a blind eye to the oppressive or discriminatory aspects of the Church just so I could benefit from faith? Justin paused.

'Yeah? Yeah,' he seemed to agree. 'That is a really real question, and it's hard to know. I don't know what the answer is.'

Despite being a woman in a heterosexual relationship, I feel like I have a slightly bigger objection to the Church's position on LGBT+ people than its position on women. I don't think there needs to be a hierarchy of discrimination, but it feels to me that, at the moment, the Church's position on same-sex relationships is weaponised against LGBT+ people slightly more than the Church's sexism is against women. Justin was the reverse and said his 'single biggest issue' was the way the Church treats women. And he had little hope of it improving. If anything, he believed it is getting worse.

'It was a much more liberal and diverse Church 20 or 30 years ago than it is today. It is being pushed further and further to the right,' Justin said. 'I think probably people like us who decided they don't like how the Church treats women, they don't like how the Church treats gays – they just left. Instead of hanging in there and trying to change it, they said, feck this. They just left.'

Almost all of the people I've spoken to who are either in the Church or have a close understanding of it have suggested that a lot of the young men joining the priesthood now are ultra-conservative. I guess this makes sense. If you're a young person who has been horrified by progressive policies, maybe the Catholic Church seems like a warmer house. Justin also agreed that a lot of the new priests were quite right wing, but made an unusual point: he said a lot of them are gay.

'I could count on one hand the number of straight priests that I know,' Justin said. 'There is something weird about an organisation that attracts so many gay seminarians, who are basically struggling with their sexuality. And that's not homophobic. That is just a weird quirk of whatever is going on the seminary system that seems to attract people who have really big problems with identity.'

'Like internalised homophobia?' I asked.

'Yeah, totally.'

He added that attitudes against reforming the Church's position on LGBT+ people manifested itself in two ways. 'Either you have the right-wing crazies who are completely, totally, vocally anti-gay, or you have the liberal priests who have it both ways.

'Why would any of us, in this day and age, join an organisation which is basically a dictatorship? Like, my parents' generation got their education from the Christian Brothers. Basically, as a result of Church intervention, they got an education. And suddenly, armed with an education, you're told, "Actually, we're not interested in your opinion. We're not interested in hearing what you think." And the way this works is, we tell you what you can think, what you should do and how you should behave. And there's no feedback upwards. You're not going to tell them your views. Why would you join an organisation like that?'

I was silent for a few seconds. All I could muster was a weak, half-hearted 'Yeah?'

It was a strong and fair point. It was also the position that I held comfortably for a number of years. Justin made the point that the Church holds zero credibility on child-protection issues. He quoted his mother, who challenged the Church's repeated failing to hold abusers to account by asking, 'Do you really believe that everyone behaved that stupidly by accident?'

I felt challenged. Laid out so plainly, it felt hard to justify my yearning to go back. Justin believes that the Church has backed up those with certain political views about LGBT+ people for a long time, and it feels the need to keep things that way because they are the people who sometimes appear to be most strongly behind the Church. Desperate to salvage some hope, I squawked out a little question. 'Do you think it will ever change?'

He sighed. 'I suppose, I have spent so much time in Rome now that I've become really cynical. It's very easy for me to sit here and do a hatchet job on the Church because there is just so much ammunition. I always ask myself: am I contributing anything here, or am I just moaning and having a rant? I'm always trying to think of what positive contribution I can make to the discussion. The fundamental stumbling block is that you're dealing with an institutional Church, which has a roadblock up and won't let you have an opinion.'

I confided in Justin that I was nervous about giving my opinion, of talking about all of this and writing this book. I was worried about the Iona Institutes of the world, who have let themselves become the default spokespeople for the Church and would probably be primed to attack someone like me.

'You know, David Quinn has just as much of a right as you or I to be talking about the Church,' Justin said. 'All you need is to be baptised, and you have just as much of a right to question the Church as anyone else.'

Justin, like me, grew up with the Church. He was an altar boy too and has fond memories of mass. We talked about how the generation coming behind us won't know that because there simply won't be enough priests available, never mind questions about who will still be going to church. I felt like I could hear the death knell.

I was glad that Justin's argument against the Church was so strong. I didn't want to just cheerily consult liberal clergy who thought I should go back to the faith. Justin knew the Church much better than I did, and if he still held those reservations then I should seriously consider them. The things he was saying were seriously challenging.

———— ✤ ————

The way the Catholic Church talks about LGBT+ people is a big deal to me and one I find hard to get past. Even if the Church reformed its poor policy on sex education, its habit of interfering in the lives of LGBT+ people would still creep me out.

When Catholics defend the Church's position on LGBT+ people, they talk a lot about 'respecting beliefs'. It's a way to make people like me sound immature, at best, or vicious persecutors of Catholics, at worst. It makes the prospect of reform seem unreasonable or even cruel, as if the likes of me are trying to force people to accept the arguments for marriage equality or equal rights. But trying to varnish the Church's position with this gloss of respectability relies on the Catholic Church being passive in its objection to gay people

– as if it was just clerics sitting in their parochial houses, poignant and composed in their respectful disappointment at all the fun same-sex weddings happening all over Ireland. But the Church isn't passive in its objection to gay rights at all.

In 2018 the Pope came to visit Ireland. Some clerics suggested to me this visit was planned shortly after Ireland voted to legalise marriage equality in 2015. I wonder if the Vatican saw it as a rescue mission or a guilt trip. As part of this World Meeting of Families event in Dublin, an exhibition was planned in the RDS. Various Catholic groups were invited to apply to have a stall at the exhibition. One of the groups was called We Are Church, a lay Catholic group in favour of the Church reforming its position on women and LGBT+ people.

The exhibition was due to be held in August. We Are Church applied for a spot in February and paid a deposit. And then, in the fine Catholic tradition of trying to ignore a problem until it goes away, We Are Church was roundly ignored for five months. Despite phoning the organisers every two weeks, nobody bothered to get back to the group – even on 5 June, when the World Meeting of Families sent out a circular mentioning that spaces were still available! We Are Church concluded fairly that its position on reform had made it unwelcome. This came after it emerged that pictures of same-sex couples in a leaflet prepared for the event by the World Meeting of Families had been replaced with pictures of heterosexual couples. And a reference to never excluding couples who did not fit the Church's view on marriage was also deleted. This seemed pretty cowardly to me. The way We Are Church was treated said plenty about the Church's thoughts on LGBT+ people, but I thought it was notable that no clerics seemed to have the balls to state it directly. If the Church is so sure of its policy that gay people are 'intrinsically disordered', why not just say it out loud?

Right when I was in the middle of my quiet state of turmoil about my own faith, I'd been working on a story that taught me a lot about what the Church does to gay people. Less than a year after the referendum on the Eighth Amendment, I'd discovered a story about an organisation called Courage International. It's a Vatican-approved Catholic group that runs what it likes to fashion as 'support groups' for people who are gay. Basically, it's a way for the Church to teach people not to get into same-sex relationships. I had found some evidence that Courage International was running meetings in Ireland.

While researching the story, I found a booklet called 'Same Sex Attraction: Catholic Teaching and Practice' written by Fr John Harvey. Fr Harvey, who died in 2010, founded Courage International. It started as a 'support group' for LGBT+ people in New York in the 1980s. Courage is now an approved apostolate of the Church and has chapters all over the world.

What Fr Harvey has written about LGBT+ people gives a good insight into what the ethos of Courage was like when it was set up. Right from the first few pages, in cold, authoritative language, Fr Harvey talks about how a 'good clinical psychologist or psychiatrist' would need to make a 'prognosis' for a gay person. A person who is homosexual is constantly described as 'a person with SSA [same-sex attraction]' as though they are a person with a disease.

He also adds that transgender people have a 'special psychological problem'. Pages and pages and pages are devoted to this kind of perverse pseudo-scientific homophobia. Being homosexual is 'selfish and self-gratifying'. Same-sex couples don't serve the common good. Homosexual relationships 'lack unity'. Gay people have 'unmet needs'. Men who are homosexual 'harbour self-hatred', it said.

'He hates himself profoundly, often drowning himself in alcohol or contemplating suicide.' This line I find particularly offensive, once you consider the very real threat this kind of Vatican-endorsed homophobia can pose to the mental health of LGBT+ people.

'The mainstream media, unfortunately, has become complicit in this political manoeuvring and commonly likens the situation of persons with SSA to that of blacks in the American South prior to the civil rights movement,' it said, railing against the notion that same-sex marriage is a civil right. According to the imprint page, this document was copyrighted in 2007. You'd never know with the Church – it could have been written fifty years or five weeks ago.

There are over 40 pages of this stuff, and I'm astounded that someone could be so righteous in their hatred of LGBT+

people that they would take the time to write such a homophobic manifesto. All the classics are in there: claims that men experience same-sex attraction because they had fraught paternal relationships and confuse same-sex attraction with wanting to be close to their fathers; they were 'over-weaned' by their mothers; or they experienced emotional abuse or sexual trauma.

There are the usual homophobic tropes about all gay men being promiscuous, and sex between men happening in 'squalid circumstances' like public toilets.

Not content with attacking LGBT+ people, their families also come under fire: 'One may suggest that very few persons with SSA come from homes where the parents, by mutual love, have created an atmosphere of caring for each child.' It said that LGBT+ people shouldn't be allowed to teach.

There are, of course, the attempts to coat the Church's homophobia in a veneer of morality – talking about how the Church wants people to be 'freed from slavery of homosexual desires' with the same kind of twelve-step programme used for alcoholics. In fact, Fr Harvey repeatedly compares LGBT+ people to those suffering with drug addictions – in a stigma-loaded way that is offensive to both gay people and those with addiction problems.

It's unmistakable: the way that this man talks about LGBT+ people is horrifying. As I read it, I was disturbed by the way he tried to intellectualise ignorance. Most right-thinking people can see the wrong in bare-faced hatred of gay people. But when it's dressed up as an act of charity, with shaky citations for its disgusting ethos, this kind of homophobia feels even more dangerous. It's not just personal, it's a policy.

In any other organisation in the world, this would be outrageous. Fr Harvey would be a pariah. That these kinds of views were not just tolerated, but promoted, would, at minimum, cause serious introspection and remorse. But the Catholic Church doesn't just accept the views of people like Fr Harvey; it actively promotes and teaches them. And even among wider society, there seems to be something that creeps close to ambivalence about the Church's appalling position on LGBT+ people. I suppose our expectations of it are so low that it's hard to get that exercised about the prejudice.

'Hate the sin, not the sinner' has a lot to answer for. The Church is audacious in its homophobia, but finds neat little ways to dress it up as something more innocent and altruistic. I can't help but feel that while the Church's views on LGBT+ people remain as archaic as ever, it has definitely become cleverer in how it frames its teachings on gay people now that society has changed. I suspect this is why the Church tries to emphasise how it believes that homosexual orientation isn't the sin, the homosexual act is. It's a marginally more PR-friendly way to threaten LGBT+ people with eternal damnation. God will only hate you if you have sex.

In a similar vein, the Catholic Church is emphatic when it says that Courage International is not conversion therapy.

Conversion therapy, which is widely regarded as wrong, relies on trying to force gay people to become straight by the end of the process. Courage International tries to get gay people to suppress their sexuality and embrace chastity instead. Kind of half-baked conversion therapy, if you like. This seems to me like a slippery way to try to give the Church's homophobia an air of respectability.

Fr Harvey did write in his booklet that gay men should be 'encouraged to move towards heterosexual inclinations by chaste friendships with heterosexual persons'. But Courage International insists that it never tries to make people eradicate their attractions or sends them for therapy. But if that's true, so what? The danger of Courage International is that it starts from exactly the same point as the most extreme kinds of conversion therapy: with the view that being gay is disordered behaviour that needs to be corrected.

The Church is pious when people challenge it on things like Courage International. I have no doubt that the people running those programmes believe they are helping people, who more often than not are probably LGBT+ Catholics who come to meetings willingly because they believe they need to control their same-sex attractions.

But I don't buy that as an excuse either. People who are LGBT+ wouldn't believe there was something fundamentally wrong with them if major organisations like the Vatican weren't helping to create societal homophobia. If a young Irish woman had been indoctrinated to believe that she was a heathen slut for getting pregnant before marriage, and waltzed willingly into a Magdalene laundry for a dose of atonement, would the fact that she went there by choice excuse the institutional misogyny of the Church? Of course not. This is why I don't like the photo-ops of LGBT+ Catholics meeting the Pope. It doesn't look to me like a meeting of equals, or even a gesture of the mutual respect they hold for their differing opinions. It looks like the Church performing an act of charity, reaching out to people at risk of 'disordered' behaviour. The Vatican believes there is only one sexuality and that is heterosexuality. It could never see LGBT+ people as anything other than people who need help. The Church is practising what it preaches through its endorsement of Courage International, and what it preaches is homophobia.

When I was working on this story about Courage International, I contacted Mary McAleese – former president of Ireland, devout Catholic and theologian. This was coming up to 12 months after the referendum on the Eighth Amendment, so I had had a full year of agonising over my faith. I didn't have the balls to tell Ms McAleese at the time, but the way she spoke about the Church galvanised me even more and pushed me closer to religion than away from it.

For me, the story was pretty clear cut. Homophobia is wrong, teaching homophobia is wrong and running courses that promote and teach homophobia in Irish parishes is also wrong. I phoned Ms McAleese at precisely the agreed time.

I don't mind admitting I was nervous. I rarely prepare questions for interviews, usually because I know the story well enough, but I did on this occasion. As with Mary Robinson before her, I was a big fan of Mary McAleese when I was a little girl. I thought having 'the two Marys' as our presidents when I was growing up was the height of glamour and, I confidently assumed, precisely the kind of 'girl power' that Geri Halliwell was always going on about in the magazines.

After Ms McAleese picked up the phone, I garbled my thanks for her offering to talk to me for the story and probably apologised for everything from taking up some of her time to even existing. I dutifully read out my first question. When Courage International frames itself as being a support group, rather than conversion therapy, is this a clever way to hide the fact that it is much closer to the latter than the former?

'Well,' Ms McAleese said, in her relaxed Belfast accent, 'I think it's slick. I don't think it's clever, I think it's Machiavellian. I think it's dangerous. It's deliberately specious. It's deliberately using language to disguise what it's doing.'

From the second she started that first answer, I couldn't have stopped her talking if I tried. Relentlessly, forensically, almost mercilessly she went through every single defence or reason the Church could have for its teaching on LGBT+ issues and ripped them all to pieces. She explained how Courage International and its practices are carefully designed to make the teachings of the Catholic Church seem legitimate, and even to flatter them. Ms McAleese pointed out that the people likely to be going to these meetings were probably devout people vulnerable due to their worry that their sexuality was a sinful, terrible thing. 'They are people who are inclined to be worried ... and who believe these weasel words, the snake-oil words, which tell them that these feelings, this idea that they have that they are gay, is something that can be changed.'

She said this teaching had to be challenged because 'the potential for damage is horrific' due to the serious mental-health threats that young LGBT+ people could face from 'ambient homophobia'.

It's an embarrassing thing to admit now, but I was struck by how unapologetic Ms McAleese was in her agitation for change. Of course, she had nothing to be apologetic for. But at the time, I believed the Church's position on LGBT+ issues had been permanent enough to almost be a divine tradition at this point. Despite being clear myself on the wrongs of homophobia, I felt that kind of prejudice was an unchangeable thing when associated with a religion. But here was Ms McAleese rallying for reform without any watery addendums or qualifications for 'respecting different beliefs'. She was crystal clear. The Church's position was wrong, and it should change.

A question that is snarled at Mary McAleese a lot is, if she doesn't like the Church that much, why doesn't she just go and find another religion? This criticism was one of the reasons I was so scared to admit for so long that I wanted to be Catholic. Ms McAleese has international theology awards up to her gills and is still dismissed as though she isn't appropriately qualified to question or to criticise the Church. And if she's not allowed to question it, what hope did I have?

I see things differently now, thank God. If you interrogate the criticism of Ms McAleese a little closer, most people aren't even claiming the things she says are incorrect. People complain about *the way* she says things. Or how often she says things. Or question why she says these things. For example, in 2018 she had been due to speak in the Vatican as part of an event held there for International Women's Day every year. Cardinal Kevin Farrell, he of the Viennetta robe, refused to let Ms McAleese speak as a panellist in the Vatican. Instead, the event was moved to Rome. In her speech, Ms McAleese criticised the Church and described it as an 'empire of misogyny'. Some disagreed with her, of course. But more seemed to take offence at the strength of the word 'misogyny', as though they had wanted her to say it in a softer way. Ms McAleese is right about the failings of the Church, and that makes people uneasy. So the focus instead is placed on how she points out those failings. People don't seem far off asking her to point out the homophobia and the sexism in a more polite way.

I asked her what she says to those people who tell her to go off and find another faith.

'The Church doesn't get everything right. It's a 2,000-year-old institution, which has a long litany of getting things wrong. Including things that it had to apologise for,' Ms

McAleese said. 'The Church gets things wrong, and it admits that it gets things wrong.'

She started to explain Vatican II to me. Pope John XXIII set up the Second Vatican Council in 1959. It changed a lot of things in the Church and created an opportunity for it to engage in a meaningful way with the modern world.

'Vatican II was a very important watershed in pointing out and making the changes that needed to be made across a swathe of things, not least the organisational structure of the Church and the role of the laity,' she said. 'Among the rights of the laity that were recognised by the Vatican Council and are now translated into the code of Canon Law is the right of members, not just lay people but anybody in the Church, to draw the attention of their sacred pastors to concerns that they have about the Church.'

I had never, ever heard this before. Why would I have? The Church was never portrayed to me as an institution that could possibly change its ways. It had never crossed my mind that people like me – had I stayed in the Church – would have had not only a right but a responsibility to speak up about the things we saw as wrong or misguided or harmful.

Ms McAleese said that these concerns could be about the Church's teachings or things the Church is doing that damages it. 'Clerical child sex abuse is the classic example,' Ms McAleese said.

People like me can sometimes see Ms McAleese almost as a lone voice, because the only time we hear a devout member of the Church criticising it in such a strong, clear way is when it's a high-profile person like her. How would I have heard of or been aware of the vast number of clerics who also share her view when I wasn't even a member of the Church myself?

'Many of the things that I say about the Church have been said by many, many others – cardinals, popes, bishops, clerics, some of them more courageous. By and large they are not, as a cohort, courageous in these matters but some of them are. And increasingly, they are more vocal and more likely to speak,' Ms McAleese said. 'I look at what Canon Law tells me, as a Catholic, I am obliged to do, and one of the things it says is that if you have these concerns you have an obligation to draw them to the attention of your sacred pastors – by which they mean the bishops. And also to your fellow and sister members of the Church. So, that's what I say to those people who would raise that criticism,' she said, answering my question. 'I would say learn more about your Church: you are wilfully ignorant of it.'

Mary McAleese was not the first prominent Catholic I had heard who was questioning her faith. But she's the first one I really paid attention to. I had been carrying around this confusion about my own faith for over a year, and it had seemed that by recognising I wanted religion in my life, I had somehow managed to make myself feel emptier. Listening to a devout Catholic whom I could relate to – ideologically – felt nourishing. It was really, really exciting.

I transcribed the interview carefully and read her answer about the responsibility to call for reform of the Church over and over. Up until then, the things I had been wrangling with myself over had made me feel like a bad Catholic. I knew in my heart that I wanted to go back to the Church, but the Church and I were in major conflict over so many things.

I was worrying about betraying my personal beliefs. But a small part of me, a part that I was very afraid of, was also asking if my beliefs about social justice would make me less-than in the eyes of God. My internal monologue was chaotic. I was constantly asking and answering questions about religion in my head, and only rarely would the answers line up in a clear way before they descended into chaos again. Imagine the cacophony of an orchestra tuning up, before briefly playing together and then falling into discord again – that was what was going on in my head. Sometimes, difficult questions would rise to the top. I asked myself a couple of times if my beliefs on the rights of women and LGBT+ people would make me a less devout Catholic. I hope nobody interprets that to mean I ever believed God hates homosexuality – I don't believe that for a minute and I never have. I think we've seen from the previous bans on marriage equality and abortion in Ireland that declaring something as wrong or forbidden or morally abhorrent does have an effect, even when you are sure that it's the laws or rules that are wrong. When considering going back to the Church, I was starting from a point where I believed that I would always be less Catholic than other people because of my own beliefs regarding what is right and what is wrong. The Church was in opposition to my conscience, rather than guiding it. I always came out of these wretched rows with myself with the same conclusion – the Church is wrong about gay people, and it's wrong about women, but that will never change. I had resigned myself to thinking that I would always be a bit of a contradiction because my beliefs about LGBT+ people and women were at odds with my faith.

But what Mary McAleese was talking about was a far more radical idea: pushing for LGBT+ equality because of my Catholic faith, rather than despite it. I knew since the referendum on the Eighth Amendment that my personal views on feminism and equality were guided by my Catholic teachings on compassion and social justice – valuable life lessons I had salvaged from a religion I'd abandoned. What Ms McAleese was talking about went much further than that and made advocating for equality a Catholic value. No, more than that: a Catholic responsibility.

I loved everything about this thesis. I have mentioned how, after the result of the referendum on the Eighth Amendment, I had been bushwhacked by patriotism. I was standing in the RDS on the morning of the count, stunned at the sense of national pride I could feel swelling in my chest. This revelation about the Catholic duty to agitate for reform was creating a similar phenomenon. I suddenly saw a version of the religion that I could love completely, without any guilt, and the appeal of it was shocking. If that version of the Church could ever be real, where the senior clerics would at least listen to lay people who wanted reform, then I wanted to be a part of that very badly.

Chapter 7

I found God in the George once. In the smoking room of one of Dublin's most famous gay bars in late 2018, I once again had a little crisis of faith.

The phrase 'finding God' mis-sells the experience. The process is nowhere near as simple as I initially thought. After I first realised I was open to religion, I was mithered by it. Everyday experiences could transform into moral quandaries at a moment's notice. God, or the idea of God, would pop up when I was enjoying any number of modern heathen indulgences. It was a bit of a dose. Who has time for that kind of introspection in this day and age?

God was haunting me. 'Finding' Him was not a linear search. It was more like a mega game of Where's Wally?, if you just replaced the little red bobble hat with omnipotence.

Taking a respite from bopping, I had sauntered out into the smoking area of the George. A young guy asked me for a light, and we started chatting. I wish I could explain how the conversation moved onto religion, but you must appreciate

I'm an accomplished shite talker when I'm out.

As I was wont to do at the time, I drunkenly confessed that I was going through some anguish over my relationship with the Church.

'Me too!' he said.

'Really!' I gushed. 'Tell me more.'

He started talking and I started chain-smoking – barely registering when I finished a cigarette before fishing another out of my depleting box of Marlboro menthols. I stared at him silently as he talked. We were both extremely pissed so there was a degree of ... intensity to our discussion. You know the way the *New York Times* sometimes writes how interviews or letters have been edited for length and clarity? The following has been edited from original events based on my drunken recollection and probable lack of clarity.

'I miss the community of the Church,' this lovely stranger told me. 'I have the LGBT+ community, but I worry that I'd be betraying them if I went back.'

I was concentrating very hard on his face as he talked, but this was no mean feat after a few jars, as I was stumbling around like someone trying to maintain their balance on the deck of a ship. But I was listening!

This young man, who was also pissed but very genuine, explained how he was in a state of conflict. The Church was prejudiced against him because of his sexuality, but he was worried his chosen family in the LGBT+ community would be prejudiced against him because of his faith – for exactly the same reason I was reluctant about going back to the Church: in case it was giving tacit support to homophobic policies.

I was riveted.

This happened to me a lot around that time. I was so afraid to talk about my Catholic feelings that any time I got the opportunity I was desperate to seize it and not let it go. Once I started talking about the Church, I never wanted to stop. Me and that stranger stayed talking for the best part of an hour as I batted away quizzical glances from friends.

Now, I could write my own Book of Revelations on the meaningful epiphanies I've thought I had in smoking areas while I was pissed. I am very proficient in the kind of late-night 'profound discussions' that leave me screaming into a pillow in humiliation the next day. Once intoxicated by alcohol, I can also become intoxicated by my own interesting observations – observations that somehow always turn stale and asinine once sober. Amazing how that happens.

Anyway, the next morning my head was pounding and my stomach was turning but I didn't quite reach the holy trinity of suffering by having the Fear as well. My phone dinged with the usual reconnaissance mission that follows the morning after the night before, but my mind was elsewhere. I couldn't stop thinking about my conversation with that young man.

I had taken genuine joy from getting to talk to some-one who felt similarly to me, though his relationship with Catholicism was undoubtedly more nuanced and compli-cated than mine. If I went back I would be afforded the privilege of having a Catholic wedding if I wanted to. He couldn't. And while the Catholic Church does appear to view women as lesser, my identity is not described as disordered behaviour by the Church, as this man's sexuality would be.

But I was feeling uncomfortable as well because the conversation made me feel guilty. When I talk about people going back to the Church automatically giving their tacit support to its policies, I think I'm putting a burden on LGBT+ people to account for the homophobia of their faith. Catholic LGBT+ people are facing a struggle from both sides. The prejudice the Church has against LGBT+ people is unquestionable, but prejudice against LGBT+ people who are religious exists as well – even if it is much, much lesser than the discrimination of the Vatican.

I understand why it could be hard for people to come to terms with an LGBT+ person wanting to support an organisation that preaches against them. I also think the pressures of being an LGBT+ person of faith can be unique. People expect LGBT+ people to be against homophobic religions, but we seem to expect nothing of the homophobic religions themselves. Criticism of LGBT+ people who support a religion like Catholicism that doesn't criticise the Church itself feels to me like it's holding the people most likely to suffer from homophobic policies responsible for them. Certainly, if I am feeling guilt about going back to the Church as a straight woman, then I can't imagine how difficult that decision could be for a person who is LGBT+.

I started to read up on this more and came across the term 'activist church-going'. Now, I know that phrase is going to make conservative Catholics' eyes roll right out of their heads. I know that not everything needs to be viewed through the prism of woke and virtuous activism, and sometimes going to mass really is just going to mass. But I am very taken with the idea of LGBT+ people being strong members of their parish and existing there in a way that is neither apologetic nor ashamed. So much of the Church's backwards stance on LGBT+ people seems to be based on pretending they don't exist at all. This is totally different to the presence of LGBT+ people in photo-ops with the Pope, which could be framed on the Vatican's terms. I want more LGBT+ people in church on their own terms, existing within the Church without needing to endorse or support an archaic policy that describes them as disordered. In that context, the mere presence of LGBT+ people in a church seems radical to me.

When I started to tell a small number of people that I wanted to be religious again, they would jokingly suggest I had 'come out' as Catholic. It was a well-meaning comment, with no malice intended, but I would never use that phrase for what I was doing. LGBT+ people have been made to feel the need to 'come out' for no good reason. I was initially embarrassed to be outwardly Catholic for what I thought were plenty of good reasons.

As I've spent more time talking to Catholics and talking about Catholicism, I've changed my view. I feel less inclined now to place the burden of accountability for the Church's wrongs on the shoulders of individuals who still choose to go. It's like climate change: it doesn't make sense to focus all of our efforts on guilting the individual for using plastic bottles when there are larger mass polluters doing much more damage. The Church's poor reputation and its devotion to archaic and dubious beliefs come from the top down.

What makes me uncomfortable is that Catholicism is one of the strands of Christianity that is clinging very tightly to a position which oppresses LGBT+ people. There have been lots of equality movements in Christian Churches across the world, and Episcopalians and Presbyterians will ordain members of the LGBT+ community. Catholicism's opposition to gay people is so strong that it's almost a defining feature of the faith, and I hate that.

— ☘ —

Almost two years on from the referendum in 2018, I took a train to a small rural town. I was meeting a woman who was a Church of Ireland priest, and she had kindly agreed to talk to me about her faith and what Christians should be doing for asylum seekers.

She had driven a considerable distance to meet me in this little town, in the lobby of a country hotel. We'll call this woman Alice. It's not her real name, for reasons which will soon become obvious.

I spotted her ensconced in a plush armchair in the hotel lobby. She had an open and friendly face. People were dotted all around us having tea and sandwiches, so she suggested that we go into the bar where it was quieter.

Alice was an understated woman who initially seemed quiet, if little giggly. We ordered tea and toasted sandwiches. She looked like she was in her early 60s, but from the dates in the stories she told me, she must have been closer to 70.

It was around noon, so the bar was deserted. Still, she led us over to the farthest corner and chose a small table well away from the bar, where a couple of teenage staff were lolling about. When we sat down to talk, she was a bit skittish. 'Is it alright if I talk to you anonymously?'

'Um, sure ...' I said. I wasn't sure what it was she had to tell me about the Church of Ireland that would prove so controversial that she had to hide her identity.

'Why don't you start?' Alice said.

I launched into what was now a well-versed spiel: how I used to feel about religion, my initial shock when that changed and the remaining concerns I had about the Catholic Church – mainly about its treatment of abuse survivors, women and LGBT+ people. She nodded excitedly when I mentioned the Church's opposition to marriage equality.

She leaned in close to me. 'Well, I belong to that particular group,' she said, laughing softly. 'I'm lesbian. And that would be ... unusual in the Church.'

As I said, she was an understated woman. I stared at her in shock. 'Is that …?' I didn't want to say 'allowed', but she picked up what I meant.

'The people I want to know, know. It's not broadcast all around the place. My bishop knows! And ordained me, despite it,' Alice said. 'Well, not despite it – you know what I mean.'

'Really! Why did you tell him?' I said.

'It was before I joined and I thought I'd rather get it over with and be turned down before I started, than get chucked out afterwards,' Alice said.

She described how she told her bishop she was gay; just came right out with it and then said, 'Is that going to be a problem?' I was starting to think Alice was a bit of a badass.

'And the bishop said, "Not as far as I'm concerned, absolutely not,"' Alice said. She said his only slight worry was that if in future she had a partner who moved into the rectory with her, it might upset some of the older parishioners. But they could cross that bridge when they came to it.

What she described sounded like such a normal response that it almost brought a tear to my eye. Would it be so hard for other Christian leaders to just … not be so weird about other people's sexuality?

The Church of Ireland, as you can see from Alice's existence as a priest, is already much more progressive than the Catholic Church. It started ordaining women in the 1990s, but it's still technically against LGBT+ rights. The Church of Ireland's position is that marriage is between a man and a woman, but it's not as passionate about the issue as some of our Catholic leaders. In 2015 the Church of Ireland decided not to campaign for a Yes or No vote in the marriage equality referendum and said it was leaving it up to parishioners to vote with their consciences.

Alice explained to me that any time the Church of Ireland's synod tries to change its position on the issue, clergy from the south tend to be voted down by clerics from Northern Ireland. There are more of them, Alice said, and they tend to be a more conservative. Still, the fact that Alice isn't out to all of her parish shows that the Church of Ireland may not be quite ready for out and proud lesbian priests. Of course, we all know that the Catholic Church has LGBT+ clergy as well. The difference is they'd be much less likely to chat to me about it over a toastie.

Alice told me that she'd been really nervous going through the selection process to be ordained. While her bishop had been super supportive, she wasn't sure who else would be on the panel and whether they knew she was gay and what their views would be. Her bishop picked up on her nerves.

'He said if anyone has any other questions to just refer them to him, and I thought that was so supportive,' Alice said.

Alice told me she had been raised Catholic, but decided to switch. It was my turn to lean forward when she said that. 'Tell me why you changed?' I said.

'A bit like yourself,' she said, taking a bite of a little triangle sandwich and then seamlessly diving into a fascinating life story. In the late 1960s, Alice got married when she was 19 years old to a man who was 21. She describes both of their decisions to wed as an 'escape-from-home situation'. They moved to another country and had two children. But, eventually, they split up once the children had grown up. 'We're still great friends,' Alice said. 'He remarried, and that's when I came out.'

'Wow,' I said, 'and had you known before?'

'Only in the latter years, after we separated,' Alice said. She went to study with the Open University after her divorce. There were lesbians in the year ahead of her, whom she got pally with. 'Then the penny dropped,' Alice said. 'It answered so many questions, all the way back to my teens.'

I had only known this woman six minutes at this point, but no matter how personal my questions were she was still happy to answer. Alice said that when she moved back to Ireland, she tried to get involved in her local Catholic Church but was basically dismissed because of her divorce.

At the time she was working as a psychotherapist in Dublin. It was the early 1990s, and shortly after she came back to Ireland the Fr Brendan Smyth story broke. Smyth was a notorious paedophile priest based in Northern Ireland whose appalling crimes were covered up by the Church.

'I was inundated with women, not all who had been abused by clergy, but who had been abused and felt for the first time that they could speak out because it was finally being talked about,' Alice said. 'I had case after case. And every time, I was hearing over and over again that they'd go to talk to their priest, after they had been abused, and the priest would say, more or less ...' She sighed. 'The priest would imply that they were the sinful ones, and they'd need to ask for forgiveness, and then they'd be fine.'

I could feel my face creasing in disgust. Alice put both her hands on the table in front of her and seemed to be struggling to articulate her outrage.

'I was getting so – Ellen, I was getting – I absolutely could feel the anger in me. In psychotherapy it's really important to keep your emotions out of the room. But that was getting very hard for me,' she said.

I thought that was such a lonely image. The devout Catholic, listening to a survivor reveal the heartlessness of the Church and trying to keep her face neutral.

'The final straw was a lovely lesbian, who was 68 but looked about 108. She was tiny, and she was frail, and she was dying of cancer,' Alice said. 'She came to me because of the redress they give them, the ones who had been in the Magdalene laundries – they let them have five counselling sessions,' Alice said, holding up five fingers tartly as though to illustrate this measly offering. 'She was going to solve forty-odd years in a ghastly Magdalene laundry in four or five sessions? I just thought ... that's it. That is it. And I left.'

I've been deliberately putting off talking about the abuse. Every time I think about it, it depresses me to the point of stupefaction. The horror of it makes any critical arguments or moral debates about going back to the Church seem pointless by comparison. It's a part of the Church that I find very hard to look at. I will get to it.

The scale of child sex abuse and the disgusting acts of self-preservation that followed are one of the most common reasons people have for leaving the Church. And who on earth could blame them?

Magdalene laundries are well known for incarcerating young women who had dared to have sex before marriage, or in some cases had the grave misfortune of being a rape victim. There are also recorded cases of lesbians being sent to the laundry, as this lady who Alice had been trying to counsel had been.

After that, Alice didn't go to church for years. She still had her faith and prayed privately. She moved to the west of Ireland and, one day, was asked to help out with some music for the local Church of Ireland. It started from there, and now she's a priest.

Alice talked to me about LGBT+ people in the clergy. She joined what started as a Bible study group with some nuns, but it slowly evolved into a support group where the women vented their frustrations with the Church. After one of the nuns' parents died, the nun came out and married her partner!

I had to ask – didn't the opposition to people like her annoy her, whether it was coming from the Catholic Church or the Church of Ireland? 'Like,' I said, 'sometimes I worry that they've made homophobia a Catholic value?'

'Oh, they have,' Alice said. 'My view is: God created us. I have no doubt that God created me, too. And his word is love. And love accepts everything, love is equality. So I have always, always felt I can get things wrong or do things wrong. But that I would be any less loved by God because I happen to be gay? No. I don't believe that.'

Alice told me, conspiratorially, that she had worked out a way to do illicit same-sex weddings. She even had one coming up a few days later.

'How d'you manage that?' I said.

One day a loyal parishioner told Alice that he had met the love of his life, and he wanted to get married. He hoped Alice would do it. But she couldn't, not under the Church of Ireland rules. Alice was heartbroken; the weight of the disappointment hung around her for days. She was in Dublin at the Church of Ireland theological institute and confided in a senior member of the Church about her problem. He gave her a meaningful look. 'Well, what I would do, or could do in that situation …'

Across the table from me, Alice laughed. 'He'd obviously done it loads of times before,' she said.

This is the secret same-sex marriage method. First of all, you need an interfaith minister who can bless a same-sex couple's civil wedding. Then, this cleric explained to Alice, the night before the civil wedding, he invites the same-sex couple and their immediate family to the church. They go through some prayers and blessings from the service, but the entire time he is secretly performing a marriage under the guise of a rehearsal.

'He marries them with God's blessing,' Alice said.

My hand flies to my chest and my mouth drops open. The romance of it! The subterfuge! Viva the gay-resistance clerics.

This man told Alice that the next day he goes to the civil wedding performed by the interfaith minister. 'Actually, makes a point of going to it,' Alice said. He told her that he's usually asked to say grace before the reception dinner.

'You know,' he told Alice, 'you can make grace as long as you like.' So he slips in another blessing for the couple into the prayer before dinner. Then he tells the couple to come back to church the first Sunday after their honeymoon. When they do, he gets the parishioners to give them a round of applause and welcome them back.

So, that's the method that Alice uses now as well. This is a major risk on the part of both Alice and the mystery cleric, and however many other Church of Ireland clerics may be doing it. I struggle to understand how anyone could see the kindness, thoughtfulness and Christianity of these illicit marriages as evidence that any of these clerics should go to hell.

Alice is sceptical about the prospect of any of the newer Catholic priests being rogue gay-marriage celebrants. Echoing what Justin McAleese told me, she said she's worried about the new clerics around my age, who qualified for

Maynooth under Pope Benedict. 'And they are *way* back,' Alice said, gesturing over her shoulder, 'pre-Vatican II.'

'Out of interest,' I said, 'what would be the difference in actual worship if I switched to the Church of Ireland?'

Alice shrugged. 'Practically nothing.'

I know what you're thinking. It sounded to me like the Church of Ireland would suit me better, too. And that's thrown at people like me a lot: 'You should go off to the Church of Ireland altogether, with your women's rights and your equality.' Some feel that people like me are just Christians with notions, and if the Catholic Church is too backwards for us then there are other options. Unfortunately, it's not like I'm trying to change my mobile-phone provider. Lapsed as I am, I am a Catholic. It is just who I am and what I am. It feels as permanent to me as my nationality, which is not something I would ever consider changing.

When I asked Justine McCarthy the same question, she'd looked back at me with pleading eyes. 'But I don't want to be Protestant!' she said.

I don't want to be Protestant either! (No defamation against Protestants intended.) I was raised Catholic. I want to be, and remain, Catholic. There's an element of sentimentality to it, of course, but what's wrong with that? It's a matter of heritage and identity. It's also a matter of principle.

I'm afraid when I hear Alice say the Catholic Church is becoming more conservative – it scares me to think it may be too late. Pushing people like me out because of matters of conscience like LGBT+ rights has created a vacuum for right-wing values to take over. So even beyond my selfish desire to remain part of the Catholic Church, I have also come to believe there is a moral argument in favour of people like me staying in.

I know full well that my search for religion must be, in some weird way, a product of my environment. Over the last few years, Irish society has constantly and repeatedly rejected the more conservative aspects of the Catholic Church's teaching. Support for the Church appears to be going one way. There is broad agreement that the Irish Catholic Church should never return to the infallible and mighty position it held in Irish society, immune to scrutiny. But by the time I went to meet Alice, it seemed possible that we were swinging so far the other way that there could genuinely be no Irish Catholic Church within my lifetime. Or worse: it would exist, but only as a small and derided institution defined almost exclusively by the things it opposes rather than the things it promotes. And I didn't want that. I don't want to watch the religion fail. Or worse, turn really nasty.

But before I could decide for sure, I had to force myself to look at the very, very worst part of the Catholic Church. The most painful and inexcusable part. And the most compelling reason to not go back.

Chapter 8

'OK,' I said, smoothing out the page of my notebook and getting my pen ready. 'Why don't you start by telling me where you're from?'

Silence. I looked up and across the table at the middle-aged man sitting opposite.

'Oh,' he said, looking a little embarrassed. Another beat passed and he smiled apologetically. 'I – I don't know.'

It was my turn to look embarrassed. 'Oh God, I'm so sorry, Jerry,' I babbled. 'I didn't –'

'Ah,' he waved away my apologies and grinned, 'you weren't to know.'

I could feel my throat catch as I busied myself with my notes, trying to get the interview back on track. Jerry was a survivor of clerical child sex abuse, and he didn't know where he was from because he had spent 18 years in different religious institutions when he was growing up. I should have known that – it was a stupid question, and I was upset with myself for asking it. We carried on with the interview

– it was for a newspaper article I was working on – and he told me about some terrible, terrible things he had survived. Still, even after I left and was walking down Jervis Street in Dublin on a hot, bright day, it was how he'd answered that first question that I kept thinking about. He didn't know where he was from – imagine that.

Any time I've interviewed survivors of child sex abuse, it seems to be the smaller, unexpected details that shake me completely. I know that sounds silly once you imagine the kinds of horrors the survivors disclose. But it's because it's always the scale and breadth of the legacy of the abuse that terrifies me. I hear people like Jerry, a 57-year-old grandfather of four, telling me he does not know where he's from, and I imagine the abuse as this big monster that can still reach its disgusting tentacles into the innocuous and the everyday, decades and decades after the attack.

Another survivor who helped me out a lot with a story over a number of months was an elderly man who loved to talk on the phone. Sometimes I felt like he was phoning me with superfluous details just to have an excuse to chat. I wish I'd been tactful enough to figure out a way to say he could call any time without embarrassing him. I didn't want him to think I was suggesting he was lonely or taking pity on him. I wouldn't have been because I loved talking to him as well.

He was such a good source – meticulous and forensic with the notes and details he'd give me as little tips for stories

– and he took the whole journalistic process very seriously. 'I could have had your job!' he'd always say.

When his name came up on my phone I would skulk into the editor's office, which was always vacant. (He was more of a 'pace around the office and talk at you' kind of editor.) I'd throw myself into the large black leather office chair and swing around in it for ages as me and this man chatted away. He liked to talk about football a lot, something I know nothing about. I'm from Munster so I always had a lot more *meas* in hurling. One day we were joking about the All Ireland football final, and I teased him, saying he'd be 'better off if he got into a real sport, like hurling'.

'Ah, no,' he said, his voice suddenly a lot softer. 'The Christian Brothers used to make us make sliotars, so I've always found hurling hard to enjoy.'

I could feel the colour drain from my face. There it was again, the vicious grasp of those ugly tentacles. An older gentleman, in the autumn of his life, deprived of the simple joy of a sport because of those disgusting people. My hand felt sweaty as I held the phone to my face. I thought I was going to choke on the emotion.

'I'm sorry,' I said. He changed the subject.

Another day, I was working on a story from a small office in Leinster House. I was tucked into a room tacked onto a small corridor. The press gallery inside the Dáil chamber runs along the left-hand side of this corridor, and pokey little offices like the one I was in run along the right.

Leinster House hums all the time. There's the drone of politicians on various TV screens broadcasting the feed from the chamber into our little offices. The voices of these TDs fail to compete with bulletins coming from phones and radios. The ancient corridor outside shakes as the feet of harried reporters pound up and down, while the furious tippity-tap of laptop keys provides a frenzied bassline for the whole symphony of the place. I was in a rush to file, so I had my phone headphones in so I could quickly type up the quotes from the woman I was talking to as we spoke.

I was writing a piece about Magdalene laundry survivors who had inexplicably been left waiting for years to access the redress they were rightfully owed by the Irish State. A woman who had survived one of those awful institutions was still, in her later years, having to advocate for herself.

'Hello,' she said.

I was surprised. Her voice was crisp, clear and sounded nothing less than 100 per cent American. Oh, I realised, of course. Once she had been let out of the laundry, this lady didn't hesitate to leave the country as well. Ireland had been nothing but cruel to her. Plenty of survivors had also mentioned how, once they got out of the laundries, they feared that they might be put back in. It felt safer to leave. Once you have been effectively banished from Irish society, I imagine, it doesn't feel too drastic to banish yourself from Ireland altogether.

This woman had lost her accent. I started to listen closely to her, the bustle of Leinster House silenced. I stopped typing and pressed on my earbuds so I could make her voice louder. I listened to the rhythm and the cadence and the tone of it. Her voice made me feel very lonesome and very far away.

I interviewed another laundry survivor in the café of a city centre hotel one day. Over tea, we talked all about the heinous abuse she suffered. I let her leave first so I could settle up, and a young waitress came over in her black waistcoat and pristine white shirt to clear the table. I had put away my dictaphone at this point.

She smiled at me. 'Ah, it's always nice to catch up with the gran!' she said.

Yes, I thought, that must have been what it looked like. These women look older and ordinary now. They have little balls of tissues in their sleeves and perfect perms. We had been talking intensely for a long time and at one point she had been holding my hand. Nobody watching would have had any way to know the kind of extraordinary life this woman had led. What the servants of the Church did to that woman had changed her life.

'I will always be a survivor,' the woman had said to me.

Survivors are not one homogenous group of people, who can be blurred together under the banner of one mass tragedy. And I know that survivors often have to deal with generalisations about them and what happened to them. Things have come up with a lot of the survivors I have interviewed that have taught me a lot about the process of dealing with abuse. The recovery can be a lifelong thing.

Many of the people who were forced into manual labour in Catholic industrial schools missed out on an education, so they struggle with literacy. Navigating forms for social welfare can be extremely frustrating.

Some people don't trust authority, for obvious reasons. That distrust can often extend to people like me. The media can feel like an arm of the State. Being conscious of this, sometimes when I'm writing up the stories of these people I feel as though I'm using oven gloves to handle precious glass.

The day I was talking to Jerry – a full year before I was even thinking about going back to the Church – I had gone to the Aislinn Centre in Dublin city centre to talk to a number of survivors of abuse for a piece I had been working on for *The Times*. The staff told me to just show up at a certain time and anyone in the centre at that point who felt like talking to me would.

They put me in a small private room with one table and two little chairs. One by one, people would come in and sit down and talk.

Jerry had been one of the first. He started to explain the permanent effect of the child sex abuse he had suffered in these Catholic institutions. 'I will never, ever know what it's like to wake up as a kid. That kills me,' Jerry said.

He told me how at Christmas he goes to his daughter's house and sits down to watch *Mary Poppins* and pretends he's a child. Jerry immerses himself in the film for a couple of hours and pretends he's watching it through a child's eyes. 'I try to live, I try and live the kid's dream,' he said.

People told me the most awful things. Things I could never repeat to anybody. One man came in and just burst into tears and could not speak. Some of the people were angry, others were devastated. One told me he had suppressed the memory of the abuse for decades until one day it just emerged again out of nowhere and turned his life upside down. Another man detailed how he'd arrived at a Catholic industrial school at the age of seven and was introduced to a priest on his first day. 'By the time he was finished with me, that was my life over with,' he said. Another man told me he was sent to one of the institutions at the age of two and never had a single visitor until he was seven years old. A man had shown up and said he was his older brother. The brother promised to come back the next week and take him home. The man waited. 'And,' the man said, and his body started to shake with tears, 'I never saw him again.'

After many hours that day, I came out of the centre and felt like I had been holding my breath underwater. I wanted to get down on my hands and knees in the street and start screaming.

Without the survivors in front of me, all I could think of were those faceless abusers. It does not strengthen my case for being a good Catholic at all, but I hate those people. I wished terrible things on them all, in my mind. When I have to write newspaper stories about these monsters, I feel like pounding the keys into oblivion when I write the words 'now deceased'. Death is too good for them.

A woman wrote to me before, asking me to look into a bishop who had died with a good name that he didn't deserve. I dread to think how many of those there may be. She told me about a friend of theirs who had suffered from hideous clerical sex abuse as a child at the hands of this monster. This woman wrote how she had watched this man have a breakdown later in life, once he had finally confronted what had happened to him. She said he was walking around like a shadow of his former self. 'It's difficult to watch the living, dead,' she said.

People talk about natural disasters a lot when they talk about times they have questioned God. They find it hard to marry that kind of devastation with a benevolent, omnipotent being, which I understand. I don't have an answer for it either. I think that clerical sex abuse feels like an unnatural disaster. It challenges me to believe in God when I think about what happened to these people. I can't imagine a God with any class of power deigning not to intervene to stop something so awful. I asked a priest about this when I started trying to go back to the Church, and he told me he did not see God in the abuser but in the abused. He saw abusers as the evil in the world, one of the many tragic reasons why we need faith in the first place. It's warped and twisted that these abusers were *using* faith. Other people would see abuse as heinous enough to be conclusive proof that there is no God. One of the reasons I believe I might need religion is because God does not control the individual actions of each person, and some of us want religion as a guide for life because we know that humans are capable of doing terrible things.

I don't like to talk about 'God's plan' too much, because I think it's often a theory that only the privileged among us can indulge in. There is an overall divine plan for humanity, sure, but I don't think it has mapped the specific vagaries of all of our lives. Of course I'd think life was following a heavenly script if it was working out well for me. Catholicism at its core is a classic story about the ongoing battle of good vs evil. I think about the number of clerical abusers we know about, and then I think about the number of them that we don't know about. Sometimes, it feels like too many for me to have faith in the good of the world.

And all of that comes before I think about the role played by the institutional Church. When he retired from radio, Sean O'Rourke mentioned in a newspaper interview a broadcast that he did with Archbishop Eamon Martin.

'How long do you think the Catholic Church will be haunted by the child sex abuse scandal?' Sean had asked the cleric.

'Hopefully forever,' Archbishop Martin had said.

Hopefully is right. There's a phrase we've heard throughout the last few decades, as these dreadful abusers have been dragged into the spotlight and, in too few cases, held to account: 'It's like being abused again.'

Everybody knows what the Church did for these abusers: it made an explicit choice to protect itself, rather than to protect children from paedophiles. Even in the cold light of the present day, the Vatican's child protection commission has been embroiled in controversy, as key members have quit in protest. Marie Collins was the last remaining abuse survivor in the commission when she resigned in 2017, citing the fact that clerics were still putting 'other concerns' ahead of child protection. After the atrocity of institutional child sex abuse, the Church's attempts to atone have been marred by ferocious self-preservation and a failure to offer timely redress.

It was not just the Church who did this: it was the State as well. I started working as a journalist in Ireland six years after the Ryan Report was published and sixteen years after the commission to inquire into child abuse was set up. I've still spent an inordinate amount of time writing about the failure or delay in providing redress to many of these people. A State agency called Caranua was originally set up to redistribute redress funds from the religious orders to pay for the health, housing and education needs of survivors of institutional abuse. That was its only job. But it constantly made the headlines for poor financial control when awarding cash to survivors, and questionable use of the fund for its own city centre offices and staff nights out. There were inexplicable delays in awarding money, and complaints about the way some survivors were spoken to by Caranua staff. Some survivors really hated Caranua. They were made to feel like a nuisance, and they didn't trust the organisation to handle what was really their money. Once, I was in the back of a taxi when a TD called me to talk about Caranua. When I finished the call, the driver turned around and said coldly, 'Are you writing about Caranua?'

He pulled over and, sitting in his seat, facing forward, let a very sad story spill from his mouth. He was a survivor of clerical sex abuse and he had also been struggling for years to get Caranua to help cover some of his healthcare costs. A lot of people in his life, he said, didn't know anything about what had happened to him when he was younger.

I sat and listened. One instance of child abuse is always too much. It would be heartless to look at the statistics of people who are abused as children to try to reassure ourselves about its frequency or rarity. But there is something about these kinds of moments that chills me. One of the worst parts of a job like journalism is the slow, dawning realisation that there are probably many people like this taxi man in our own lives. We know them and love them but we have no clue what kind of horrors they've masked from us.

Sometimes, people in the Catholic Church don't seem to accept that it was the establishment in Ireland. Whataboutery will often try to redirect discussion of plain and clear wrongs of the Church. With Magdalene laundries, for example, some Church defenders will ask: what about the people who willingly sent their daughters there? What about the State, which knowingly let them operate? At that point, Ireland was predominantly Catholic, and the clergy had significant leadership roles in society. If Ireland's first century had been an experiment in what a Catholic society would look like, then the religion would have been deemed a failure. Of course there was some good, but it has taken decades to uncover and atone for and try to redress the bad.

The last decade has shown a dramatic change in the way that Irish people regard Catholicism, and the Church has not always served itself well while trying to navigate this difficult period. The Church has faced an existential threat, so I have a very small amount of sympathy for it. Irish society changed from treating the Church with obedience and reverence to criticism and distrust, with good reason. When I listen to some Catholic leaders or Catholic groups, I get the impression they would like us to move on from that phase very quickly.

These sensitive Catholics will rail against any criticism and rush to point out that the Church 'did a lot of good'. Would they like an audit? It seems like a dangerous approach to me. How many positives would you need to tot up on the good side of your balance sheet to cancel out raping children on the bad side?

Some people have used the failings of the Church as licence to be flagrantly anti-Catholic. They describe the Pope as the leader of a paedophile ring, and sometimes suggest that people who support the Catholic Church are either evil or stupid themselves. That is clearly unfair, and I understand that it doesn't make any sense for the Church to try to appeal to people who have already decided it's a morally bankrupt and evil organisation. But sometimes people in the Church or lay Catholic think tanks are so sensitive to criticism that they paint everyone who has a problem with the Church as viciously anti-Catholic. It seems like evidence of a persecution complex. And that kind of response does damage because it makes those Catholics seem unfeeling about the horrible wrongs of the Church, which only serves to vindicate the original criticism.

The endemic nature of clerical child sex abuse makes me doubt the good in the world. It's a major spiritual challenge. People's faith was extorted; God was used as a grooming technique. Catholic abusers took something divine and degraded it. *Corruptio optimi pessima* – the corruption of the best is the worst of all.

One of the survivors I had interviewed that day in the Aislinn Centre still had a miraculous medal that he'd been given by a priest when he was in the industrial schools. He still believed, and he told me that he prayed every day. This was a year before I even started to think about going back to the Church, and that kind of devotion baffled me at the time. I had zero regard for the Church and still saw the organised religion as inseparable from the abuse that the institutional

Church was responsible for. I couldn't understand why this man would or could still believe. Why would he support the institution that had ruined his life?

The Church didn't deserve his support, but I shouldn't have assumed it was getting his support. If I had been through what that man had been through, I don't know if I would still believe in God. It's hard to say. While I questioned him for it before, I admire him for it now. That kind of faith is a strength.

I was slow on the uptake, but I've finally realised that it would be very hard for anyone to go back to the Catholic Church if they didn't first have their own strong, individual relationship with God. To translate it to terms that I understand in my capacity as a hun, I want my relationship with my priest to be like my relationship with my hairdresser. The day-to-day management is down to me, but I rely on them for occasional help with basic maintenance and structure.

When it comes to the scandal of clerical child sex abuse, I don't need to find passages in the Bible to help me understand what I think. I don't need a referendum result to back up what I believe. The wrong is obvious. The stacks and stacks of reports and investigations into the abuse, which can somehow be even more devastating to read about in dry legal language, make a compelling case for abandoning the Church altogether.

There is no way that I or anybody could argue with someone who decided to walk away from Catholicism for that reason. And I knew that from the moment I first sought to find religion again, which is probably why I put off thinking about the abuse for so long. Because it's really difficult.

No matter what happens between me and my belief in the future, I will probably never fully support the institution of the Irish Catholic Church. I see the institutional Church as a support for my faith, rather than a conduit. I cannot even imagine, for example, carelessly dropping some money into the collection basket on a Sunday morning without beleaguering myself with questions about what and whom my money is supporting.

I can't say what anybody else prays for when they talk to God. If others understand God the same way that I do, then there can't be many people who sit down and pray for revenge or retribution. I usually pray to get by.

As far as I am aware, my life has not been directly affected by the terror of child sex abuse. I can't get close to understanding what going through that does to your relationship with Catholicism, which is a fortunate position to be in. I think it's important to explain how I separate the abuse from the faith, and how I could justify even thinking about going back after everything that happened.

I thought about the worst thing that ever happened to me. Something terrible, which I will probably never write about in a book. Why do I still believe in God if awful things like that could happen? Because I didn't see God in that bad thing: I saw the flaws of man. And the flaws of man justify the need for religion – even when the flawed men are using religion to do evil things. I'm not just referring to the abusers themselves when I say 'evil things' – I'm also talking about the people who covered up for them.

That is why I am able to consider going back to the Church, dispute its heinous record of protecting children from the child sex abusers who hid in plain sight among its clerics. Those paedophiles were men; they were not gods. Though, for reasons which will never be satisfactorily explained, some people treated them with the impunity usually only reserved for gods.

Chapter 9

People talk about my generation as the one that shook off Irish Catholicism, citing our role in winning the referendums on marriage equality and the Eighth Amendment. That's a fair analysis, and there is certainly a possibility that people my age could be some of the last to grow up in this country almost universally with a Catholic education and a childhood peppered with memories of mass.

I think the generation that came before us deserves some attention as well. People of faith of my parents' age seemed to succeed in managing their anger at the Church with keeping their faith, which is a more impressive task than simply walking away – like I did.

In the late 90s I remember adults talking about the Church with absolute disdain in light of what was coming out. But the idea of not going to mass because of that was inconceivable. Sometimes, churchgoers my parents' age talked about the clerics who had been accessories to endemic abuse as an unsavoury conduit for religion – which everyone barely tolerated. I appreciate now how different this was to the way they would have had to talk about the clergy when they were younger. When I was small, my parents told us how the clergy used to beat them in school. I have heard some of my friends' parents, who are very devout, call nuns 'a pack of bitches' based on their childhood experiences with the clergy.

I used to see this as kind of hypocritical, but I now see it as the sign of a strong faith. Their relationship with God was separate to their relationship with the clergy.

With the benefit of hindsight and some slightly better-informed perspective, I can see that walking away from the Church in my late teens was relatively easy for me. I regret the years that I have lost now, but at the time it was no great sacrifice. The downfall of the Irish Catholic Church came when I was too young to have made practising religion the habit of a lifetime. Maybe it wouldn't have been so easy for me to walk away if I was a little older, and better understood how much value Catholicism really holds for me.

The popular narrative is that people my age are the woke ones, and we could see the moral flaws in the Church more clearly than our parent's' generation. But that's very patronising. People my parents' age were more likely to see the pressure to conceal pregnancies, the oppressive silence surrounding known abusers and the sanctimonious hypocrisy of some clerics at first hand. People my parents' age were more likely to be victims. Not everyone who kept going to mass just brushed off what happened before getting down on their knees again.

We talk a lot about the people who left the Church because of child sex abuse, and we know that some of those who stayed struggled with the issue. But I also have questions about some of the other people who stayed and may not have been as troubled by the record or direction of the Church. A lot of the people I've spoken to over the last couple of years about the Church have pointed out that it appears to be moving even further to the right.

Some priests have warned me that some of the younger men taking up the vocation seem to glorify the 1940s and 1950s, when the Church was enjoying ferocious power and influence and the evasion of scrutiny. I cannot help but feel that if that is true, then the future Church could be inhospitable to people like me.

If it has been hard for people like me, who value faith, to work out if we should stay or go, it must have been quite challenging to those who have devoted their lives to Catholicism.

It hadn't really occurred to me to think about what the last few decades had been like for the good clergy of Ireland. Had some of them left already? What if even more of them left? Who would I be left with? The very last people I considered when I thought about the consequences of abuse were the priests.

In 2010 Bishop William Lee, the former bishop of my home diocese, had been forced to apologise for his handling of child sex abuse. Bishop Lee had failed to report an abusive priest to the gardaí for two years, after two survivors first brought the priest to his attention in 1993. Bishop Lee had moved the priest to a new ministry and never told the priest's new colleagues about the allegations against him.

I would have thought that this case of a bishop apologising so close to home would be more memorable for me, but Bishop Lee was just one of many. Reading back on it now, the news stories about Bishop Lee's apology start with the words 'Another Irish bishop ...' I'm sorry to say this kind of story, at that point, must not have struck me as particularly extraordinary at all.

By 2013 a number of extensive reports had been published on child safeguarding issues in several parishes. In a pastoral letter, following the publication of the report on the parish of Waterford and Lismore, Bishop Lee again apologised to survivors of child sex abuse. 'I am truly sorry for what you have suffered and I pray that the Lord Jesus will heal you and bring hope, love and peace back into your lives,' the letter said.

A lot of these kinds of apology letters were being sent around to parishes at the time. A priest, who we'll call Fr Bourke, was reading one such letter out at his Sunday service when he broke down in tears. He had been on holiday the week before, so he hadn't had a chance to read the letter himself before he read it to the parishioners.

'A man who was a reader was sitting near me. He stood up and said, "Will I read it?" And I said, "No, just stand beside me." I just needed the physical presence of someone near me, you know? I finished it anyway, in the end. I finished reading it. But people came up to me afterwards and said how that must have been a very difficult thing to do. And I said it was! Because I didn't abuse anybody!'

From what I understand, Fr Bourke is an extremely popular priest in his parish. He is a kind and conscientious man, but he's also very funny. He had been reduced to tears in front of the parish by the legacy of child sex abuse and the shame of being associated with it. Fr Bourke couldn't understand why parish priests like him were made to read a letter of apology, rather than having it come directly from the clerical hierarchy – including those in the Church's hierarchy, like Bishop Lee, who had previously conceded their own role in covering up for child sex abusers.

'I think we were doing the dirty work, while these fellas were being protected and hidden away. It was embarrassing! It was really embarrassing,' Fr Bourke said.

It used to irritate me when people brought up the impact of the child sex abuse scandal on the good clerics of Ireland. It struck me as whataboutery, and I used to dismiss it as some sort of #NotAllPriests nonsense. This was often because these comments were made by those who seemed willing to defend the Church at all costs, no matter how wrong it had been. It left a bad taste in my mouth.

It made a big difference to hear this from someone first-hand. My heart went out to Fr Bourke.

I've said already that Catholicism appeals to me because it fits with my idea that most people are fundamentally good. For the same reason, I believe that most people who are drawn to the vocation of the priesthood are fundamentally good as well. I'm sure even some of the 'restorationists' who are apparently joining the clergy have a desire to help people too. Self-interest and cronyism seem to be more likely at the higher echelons of the Church. I had never seriously considered before how painful the last decade may have been for ordinary, good parish priests. I also didn't consider how the Church losing good people over the last few years would also include good clergy.

Fr Bourke agreed to talk to me about the concerns I had about the Church. Something told me he'd have interesting things to say. He talks very fast and has a lovely, soft voice. Within a few minutes he was chatting to me as if he'd known me my whole life. It turned out that I was thinking about coming back right when he could be about to leave.

'I'm the right man for you to be talking to, and the wrong man at the same time,' Fr Bourke said. 'I'm very much in the same boat as you. I'm looking at my days in the priesthood as numbered. I am at a crossroads in my own life, so I feel like we're singing from the same hymn sheet. So much annoys me about the Church.'

After decades of being a priest, he told me he was considering leaving. I was a bit taken aback. Why?

'Hypocrisy,' he said. 'I see hypocrisy in the Church and it just annoys me, it really bugs me. I'm struggling at the minute – that's why I decided to do this course.'

Fr Bourke told me he is trying to move into another career, something like counselling, that will really help people. Isn't that lovely? Priests, as I've learned myself, already need to be able to offer a certain kind of counsel. It strikes me that Fr Bourke obviously has a deep desire to help people, and it's upsetting that he feels that's no longer something he's able to do in the Catholic priesthood.

'I just feel that I can help people in a different way now. I think I can help more people that way, than with a collar around my neck. In a way, I've been counselling people all my life but I didn't always have the skills,' Fr Bourke said.

He told me that he already has 'all those years' experience in the bag', and having started his studies, he now believes that all priests should be made to do this sort of course anyway.

'I've given until it hurts,' the priest said. 'I just believe that the institution that Jesus handed down to Peter has been manipulated and forced and tweaked here and there to suit men. I believe that there are still cover-ups going on today, in 2020.'

Fr Bourke has watched other good people leave over the years, which has also given him pause. 'Really good lads would leave. And you'd say, well, if they leave, how good am I going to be? You kind of judge yourself on what you think of others,' Fr Bourke said. 'I'm still there, but barely hanging on at the moment, to tell you the truth.'

When I was speaking to Fr Bourke, only two priests were training for his diocese. He was almost 53, and he was one of the youngest priests in the parish. 'That's frightening,' he said. When he heard a bishop advocating for vocations one day, he thought, 'You'd want to look after the ones that you have.'

From talking to him, I get the sense that there isn't always as much strong collegiality between priests as there could be. I suppose the parish system isn't designed for it, and at times it can probably be an isolating job.

'We could be kinder to each other, really, as clergy,' Fr Bourke said.

The future looks uncertain. Even before talking about the loss of priests by quantity, think about the loss of priests by quality.

Fr Bourke brings a joy to his job. He always adds a special embellishment to occasion masses. For example, when he's doing a First Holy Communion he keeps his phone turned on in his pocket underneath his vestments. At a pre-arranged moment in the mass, a teacher will phone him. After what appears to be his initial annoyance, Fr Bourke will feign realisation before scrambling through his pockets, producing the phone and saying, 'Hello, Jesus!' For the benefit of the children, he will keep chatting away on the phone to Our Lord and Saviour while standing at the altar. The same stunt works just as well on Christmas Eve with a call from Santa Claus.

He's a very understanding man. After the advent of camera phones, there was some consternation over parents getting in the way while trying to take pictures of their son or daughter during Communion masses. Fr Bourke devised a solution whereby he would pose with each individual child and a piece of communion afterwards. 'I say to the children, "You look at the communion and I'll look at you,"' Fr Bourke said. 'The pictures come out lovely!'

When people die, Catholic priests sometimes ban certain music selections from the funeral – regardless of how special or sentimental they are to the deceased – because it's deemed inappropriate to play in a church. When Fr Bourke is doing a funeral, he tells the family to 'pick whatever'.

'I've been to funerals where a priest's parents have died, and they can have country music or Daniel O'Donnell or the whole shebang with people up in the gallery singing. But then, when a parishioner dies and the family wants a certain song, those priests won't allow it,' Fr Bourke said. 'I feel peeved by that. It's one rule for their family, and it's a different rule for others.'

He was the chaplain of a direct-provision centre in the diocese. Fr Bourke wanted to help the asylum seekers get to know the local people in the town, so he started asking parishioners to be godparents to some of the children in the direct-provision centre. 'Yeah, so there's a load of people now in [the town] and they've little black godchildren,' he said.

And then there are the weddings. Fr Bourke's weddings are legendary. I told him that a friend said that if every mass was like his wedding mass, they'd be in the church every week.

'I just want people to be able to look back on the day and say, "Wasn't the priest amazing?"'

I started laughing, and he added he didn't mean it in a 'cocky way'.

'I just want to make the day special and joyful. I don't want them to be looking up at me saying, "What in the name of God is he on about?"' he said. 'I always say at that point, I know as much about getting married as the bride. Because she's not married yet.'

Fr Bourke never had a 'bolt from the blue' or a moment of divine intervention before he decided to join the clergy. People used to tell his mother that he was a nice, quiet young boy and that 'he'd make a lovely priest'.

'It's the same as asking, why does a nurse become a nurse? In the end, I thought I could help people,' he said.

He's seen by others as a bit of a 'rogue' priest. It annoys him to be painted with the one brush used for the entire Irish Catholic Church. Fr Bourke disagreed with the Church's stance during the marriage equality referendum, for example. 'Because I'm a priest, people think they know what I'm thinking,' he said. 'But in actual fact, nobody ever asked my opinions. I would never get up and preach anything I don't believe in.'

But he's self-aware. When he criticised the Church and its hypocrisy, he added that in a way he was 'shooting himself in the foot' because there were times when he hadn't spoken out.

Years and years ago, when Fr Bourke was thinking of becoming a priest, his brother had asked him why. And he had said, 'Because by being on the inside, I can make a difference.'

'And I believe that I have made a difference in a lot of people's lives throughout the years. I didn't make a difference to the institution, but I certainly did in people's ordinary lives,' the priest told me. 'But the institutional Church, I don't agree with. I don't like the institutional Church. All that cover-up of abuse and the way they treat LGBT people and all that kind of stuff, I disagree with myself. And I can't shout it from the rooftops then, either.'

'Why do you think you can't?' I said.

'Because you're really putting yourself above the parapet,' Fr Bourke said.

Ms McAleese had explained to me that it was the responsibility of those within the Church to call out wrongs that they were aware of. I agree with her, but my heart also went out to Fr Bourke. I think it says more about the climate within the Church than Fr Bourke's character that, even after devoting his life to the faith, he still felt more comfortable leaving the clergy than he did speaking out against it.

This is very selfish of me but the thought of him leaving the priesthood makes me panic. It's hard not to worry about what kind of Church I'd be going back to. Losing clerical talent is important. I have problems with some of the people at the top of the Irish Catholic Church, but I'm not likely to have to see them every Sunday. If the Church is haemorrhaging good priests at local parish level, that is going to have a more immediate effect on people like me.

I had liked to imagine that, if and when I found my own parish, it would make returning to Catholicism easier if I had a good and understanding priest. What if he's a bad one? Or what if the hierarchy of the Irish Catholic bishops moves more to the right, as so many people have warned me? Fr Bourke told me he had some concerns about what could happen when certain archbishops retired and were replaced with more hard-line or right-wing men. Would I be a hypocrite to go back if that was the case?

'Well, I'd say to you what was said to me when I raised concerns about senior bishops years ago: if you don't like your postman, you still take your post,' Fr Bourke said. 'Take the message. Even if you don't like the priests and the people in control, take the message.'

He explained to me that the Church isn't all bad: there is a lot of camaraderie. And often it might come more from the other people in the parish than from the priest. He made dry comments about 'hypocrites' who seemed to be front at centre at most services. But in the quieter majority of the parish, there were a lot of truly Christian people.

'I'll be almost 30 years ordained now this year, and I wouldn't have lasted seven days if it hadn't been for the lay people. It was the people who uplifted us – they kept us buoyant and they were affirmative. You wouldn't want to wait to be affirmed by bishops,' Fr Bourke said. 'You will get that warm welcome as well, if you're open to it.'

There are the Fr Bourkes of the world who have left the Church, and there are the Fr Bourkes of the world who have stayed. I could hear anguish in his voice as he spoke about walking away. When he was going through all of these worries and concerns about the Church, I asked, did it ever threaten his belief in God?

'No,' he said instantly.

I have believed for a long time, but I haven't properly acted on it. I haven't managed or invested in having religion. Fr Bourke has done a lot of good in the name of God with his life. I haven't, and at this late stage I have a lot of lost time that I need to make up for. I think I want to go back. I would like to at least give it a chance.

'Nobody can do it for you, and nobody can decide for you. It's just by talking to people and getting different views or similar views,' Fr Bourke said. 'I thought I was abnormal, but with other priests, I'm feeling it as well. You could find other people who feel the same way. I think the fact that you're doing this, and you're talking to people, it shows that you might already be there. I get that sense from you. To even start doing this, I think on a very deep level – though you may not have realised it – you already had the decision made.'

He was right, I realised. I did.

Chapter 10

One of the simpler pleasures in my life is a trip to the women's bathroom. As everyone knows well, the deepest, briefest friendships are formed by two heretofore unknown soul sisters who happen to be at the sink putting on their lipstick at the same time. But I also believe the beauty of the cubicles has gone unsung for too long.

The backs of the bathroom doors are tiny archives of women's lives. You go for a wee, you stay for the gossip. I like to sit in the cubicle and read about all the fleeting romances documented in permanent marker. The best ones have addendums. A declaration that ASH LOVES MARK is sabotaged by a claim that maybe Mark or Ash or even both of them are sluts. (Who are these people whose lives are so intertwined that they all go for a wee in the same place?)

I like the ones written in lipstick because it suggests an unknown urgency. My favourites are the debates. On the cubicle wall in a pub near my house, someone has earnestly pleaded with women in neat black pen to 'BE THE GOOD

AT DIY HUSBAND YOUR MAM ADVISED YOU TO MARRY IN THE WORLD'. In one response, someone declares 'I already am!' while another rejects the original author as a 'GOBSHITE'. The most recent response, at the time of my visit, said 'no need to be mean'.

I think bathroom graffiti also puts the 'pee' into politics. Before the 2020 general election, my anthropological bathroom visits also noted some pastel-coloured stickers saying 'FUCK FINE GAEL' or 'FUCK FIANNA FÁIL' that had started to emerge. (If any psephologists would like to borrow my polling method, please feel free.) A lot of bathroom doors in Dublin are now relics of a different time – like the ones with 'REPEAL' scratched into the wood. I've seen a few cubicle doors host abortion debates. Back before abortion was legal, these private spaces in public were where women shared illicit information as well. There used to be big white stickers with a cerise pink dot in the middle that said 'SAFE ABORTION WITH PILLS'. They were advertising a website called Women on Web, which is an international organisation that finds ways to send abortion pills to women in countries where the procedure is banned. For a long time, hundreds of women in Ireland would order these drugs on the internet so they could illegally induce a termination in an early pregnancy at home by themselves. Some, who can't access a legal abortion for whatever reason, probably still do. Before the original pub was closed down, one of the women's bathrooms in the Bernard Shaw had a list written on the wall. It said, 'DO NOT CONTACT: Womenhurt.ie – antis; Abortionadvice.ie – antis; Cura – Religious.' It was a list of anti-abortion crisis pregnancy agencies. I keep a picture of it on my phone. It reminds me of a woman I met a few years ago who told me her own story about a bathroom door, and I still think about it all the time.

Let's say the woman's name is Rachel. I met her in 2017 when I was working for *The Times,* back before I was even thinking about religion. She had a story that she wanted to tell me, and she came up to Dublin especially. We met in a near-empty Library Bar on Exchequer Street in the middle of the day. In that big grand room with its plush furniture and fancy décor, we must have just looked like two pals having a catch-up. Once she started talking, she didn't stop, and I sat there and listened with my jaw on the floor.

When Rachel was in college in 2000, she read an ad on the back of a toilet door for a crisis pregnancy agency called Cura. Cura is shut down now, but it was run by the Irish Catholic bishops from 1977 to 2018. I'd seen ads for it myself – they often ran on Dublin Bus and I'd spot them on my way to work in the morning. I always noted that the adverts never made it clear who owned the agency and what its ethos was. Cura would not discuss all of your options with you. Its counsellors would never discuss abortion, even if that was what the woman wanted. Anyway, when Rachel saw it, she didn't know that it was run by the Catholic Church. She was 21, in the final year of her degree, and pregnant. She said the condom had broken. As was the case when I was 17 and under my bed scrabbling for money, the morning-after pill was not available over the counter.

She was refused emergency contraception in a clinic in Galway, where she was studying. Panicking, she got a train from Galway to Dublin, but the women's health clinic in the capital had no free appointments that day. Now in a total state, she was advised by a friend that she could access the morning-after pill in Northern Ireland. She spent what money she had left on a train to Belfast, took the pill and stayed overnight.

I was really struck by this part of the story. These were the actions of someone who not only knew that she did not want to be pregnant but had also gone to great effort to try to make sure she wasn't. Rachel told me that about two and a half weeks later, her period didn't come. She took a test and it was positive.

Rachel had to explain to me that, in the year 2000, there was a vacuum of information and finding some wasn't a simple matter of googling it. Sure, I was in college about a decade after her and I knew just as little about abortion, smartphone or no smartphone.

Rachel knew abortion was illegal and didn't know much more than that. She said one of her friends knew how to get to the UK for an abortion, but didn't want to tell her in case she 'got in trouble'. Her mother told her she needed to speak to a counsellor.

'And I remember the back of the door of the toilets in GMIT, where I was studying, had "CURA CARES" and all these signs for crisis pregnancy advice. So I thought, well, I can go there and I'll get some advice and I'll find out what are my options,' Rachel said. 'I really hadn't decided what I wanted to do. I was fucking terrified at the time, totally and utterly terrified.'

She went back home to Cork, where her family lived. She called the national Cura phone line and it referred her to the Life crisis pregnancy agency, above the Singer shop at 77 Grand Parade. 'Or Pan, as we call it in Cork,' Rachel said.

Now five weeks pregnant, Rachel sat in the tiny waiting room. Her description was really vivid and specific, even all those years later. She said she was sure she was five weeks pregnant, for example, because there had been two weeks of 'utter fucking panic' before the appointment. She started telling me about the waiting room, how she remembered seeing Southern Health Board leaflets scattered across the table. (This was five years before the HSE was founded.)

Rachel said she was brought in to see a counsellor, and she was still able to recall what she looked like: an official-looking woman wearing a navy suit and a floral top.

'I sat down and she was, like, "Well you do know now, your baby has a heartbeat." And, "You can't even think about having an abortion – that would be murder."'

This started to sound familiar. Over the past few years, I'd done a few undercover investigations into rogue crisis pregnancy agencies. Ireland didn't regulate crisis pregnancy agencies. In fairness to the State, one would have hoped that it wouldn't have needed to. Unfortunately, this created a major opportunity for some truly appalling people. Anti-abortion activists set up – and are still running – entire fake crisis pregnancy agencies. In fact, there are more of them now than ever before. They have websites and ultrasound machines and offices and receptionists and 'counsellors'. They used to name them something like the 'Aadams' centre because having a name that started with 'a' would mean they were at the top of the 'crisis pregnancy' page in the *Golden Pages*. After the advent of the internet, they started spending a fortune on Google adverts so their clinic would be the first one that a woman would see when she was looking for advice online. Google made money from these agencies and still does. And the competition for the top spot on Google means that the HSE has to spend a lot of public money trying to outbid rogue agencies to buy advertising spots on the Google search result pages.

These rogue agencies like to specifically target women who are looking for information about abortion – they only want to find women who are thinking about terminating their pregnancies. Obviously, none of them makes it clear that they are run by anti-abortion activists. In fact, most of them co-opt feminist language and allude to 'choice' in order to make the woman believe she's contacting a pro-choice agency. One Dublin-based group of anti-abortion activists specifically rented premises right beside a pro-choice agency and painted itself the same colour. It would try to intercept women who were going for a legitimate appointment with a pro-choice counsellor by offering them an ultrasound scan or an appointment for free. Appealing to a woman's economic insecurity is a favoured strategy of anti-abortion agencies both in Ireland and the US.

Once they get a woman into their clinics, the modus operandi is to scare her out of an abortion. The misinformation that the agencies use to do this varies. The worst ones claim abortions cause breast cancer, turn a woman into a child abuser, cause her organs to fall out or make her infertile. Slicker agencies run by groups with more money and marginally more cop-on use bogus 'studies' to suggest that abortion will destroy the woman, usually starting with her mental health.

These anti-abortion groups vary. Some of them are openly misogynistic; others have the good sense to shroud themselves in 'concern' for the women. They all have one single thing in common, though. They're run by 'Catholic' anti-abortion activists.

As Rachel described her appointment, I knew this was another case of some agency trying to scare a woman out of an abortion. I had interviewed a lot of women who had been in similar situations, but as she continued to talk, I realised that I had never heard a story quite like hers before.

The counsellor warned Rachel that she had probably talked to 'loads of people' about her crisis pregnancy. The counsellor told her: 'One of those people now could go to the guards and tell them that you've had an abortion. And you could, if they find out, spend years in prison. So really, your options are: you have to go through with the baby.'

This was bullshit. Not only could Rachel not get arrested for going to the UK to access a safe and legal abortion, she – like all Irish women – had a constitutional right to leave the country for an abortion. This right was added to the constitution in 1992 in a referendum that followed the X case. For about a quarter of a century, one part of the Irish constitution explicitly forbade abortion by equating the life of the foetus with the life of a woman, while another part gave us the legal right to leave the country to terminate a pregnancy somewhere else. I could live to be forever and a day and I don't think I'd ever get over how ridiculous that was. (No anti-abortion groups ever campaigned to get the right to travel repealed, by the way.)

But Rachel did not know about her right to travel, so the scare tactics worked. The counsellor also told her that if she had an abortion, the 'chance of you having a baby further down the road is very limited'. The woman told her the termination would cause Rachel's body to 'reject a foetus'. As we sat there in the library bar together, she told me how she wandered back onto the street in a daze.

'I thought, "Oh my God. Somebody thinks that I could be a murderer. Somebody thinks that I should be in prison for even thinking the way I thought,"' she said.

She genuinely believed she could have been arrested. 'And that would definitely be the end of any opportunity, and God only knows what would be at the end of it – you've got a criminal record and a prosecution. So I had the baby. That's basically it.'

That baby, she explained, was now her beloved teenage son. Of course, this is the part where the anti-abortion activists would rejoice. Wasn't this proof of everything they'd said all along? Huge amounts of power have been ascribed to the miracle of birth and the bond between a mother and a baby and, surely, Rachel would be proof of that. She did not want to be pregnant, but she had the baby and now she wouldn't give him up for the world. Some might even be thankful that the counsellor had lied to her.

Rachel told me that after she decided to continue the pregnancy solely out of a fear of being arrested, she spent her twenties watching her friends go on to achieve what they wanted, their financial security getting better and better. 'Mine tanked,' Rachel said. 'Towards the end, I did love the kicking and things like that and, Jesus, when I had him, of course I absolutely loved him. That goes without saying. I did love him. I do love him. But it is hard not to feel resentment,' Rachel said. 'Resentment that my twenties were totally given over to child inoculations and queuing in a community welfare office asking for rent allowance or begging and begging a Fianna Fáil TD for the back-to-education allowance so I was able to go back to college to do my master's. I spent my twenties doing that.'

She remembered pushing a car in the snow, alone, with a two-year-old in the back because she couldn't afford to get it fixed but desperately needed it to live on lower rent outside Galway city. There were weeks spent living on tinned beans. At one stage, she said, she developed a very real understanding of how women who do not wish to end up in sex work.

She spent over a decade fruitlessly chasing the father for maintenance, watching him graduate, get a job and travel the world. 'Watching that happen was a kind of torture I wouldn't wish on anybody else. Absolute hell. It's kind of like this indentured servitude that's dished out to women in that situation that makes me very, very angry,' Rachel said.

She said she felt she was vilified for wanting an abortion, and then she was vilified for not having it and being a single mother. 'And it really pisses me off in this country that single parents are seen as taking advantage of the system. They should have everything thrown at them, everything, because they are rearing our future on their own,' Rachel said.

Here's something that I wish I'd known a lot sooner: abortion stories are not fables. People love when a woman 'shares her abortion story' because they all end with a moral. The moral changes depending on which side you're on, because both sides will be able to find a woman who suits.

I will spend a long time reckoning with the way that the media, of which I was a complicit part, treated women's stories before the 2018 referendum on the Eighth Amendment. The women who came forward to talk were treated like two-dimensional figures of tragedy, permanently suspended in a state of grief. The trauma needed to be so all-consuming that they weren't even allowed to be the protagonist in their own story. I got to know a woman called Claire Cullen Delsol who was part of Termination for Medical Reasons. She told me how women like her almost had to be 'demonstrably fucked up' by the Eighth Amendment. There seemed to be some belief that women nearly needed to bleed live in front of the Irish public before they could be convinced to vote Yes.

Women who decide to terminate a pregnancy can obviously feel guilt and doubt without ever feeling regret. Similarly, on the other side, women who regretted terminating a pregnancy had to be consumed by their grief to the point that it defined them. Any normal human nuance was completely erased, lest it be seized upon by the other side. (That's the other problem with pro-choice or anti-abortion campaigns using women's individual experiences to fight one of the most socially contentious issues in the world: it's those women who get attacked.)

I think about Rachel's story all the time because it's the nuance of it that's the most important part. Loving a child that she had because she was scammed out of a choice didn't negate her right to be outraged by what had happened.

The other reason this story sticks with me so much is because it reminds me of all the things I don't like about Catholicism. Catholicism – whether it is led by the Church or the self-appointed protectors of 'good Catholic values' – seems to be much more willing to intervene when it comes to what it perceives as the moral ills carried out by women and LGBT+ people than any other social justice issue. There are great Catholic organisations working on social justice issues like homelessness, and it's not fair to erase their work just because some extremists have devoted their lives to running a fake crisis pregnancy agency in the name of Catholicism. The problem I have is that the Church as a whole is never as vocal and visible on issues like homelessness as it is when objecting to abortion or marriage equality.

The crisis pregnancy agencies I wrote about were run by two groups called Human Life International Ireland and the Good Counsel Network – both Catholic groups, both run by anti-abortion extremists. One Sunday night in 2015, before the first story I did about these rogue agencies came out, I was lying in bed, worrying. I felt a weird twinge of guilt. This story was about a rogue agency called The Women's Centre at 9 Berkeley Street, run by the Good Counsel Network, that we had gone undercover to have a counselling session with. The 'counsellor' claimed that abortion would cause breast cancer and turn a woman into a future child abuser – all total scaremongering rubbish. My worry was that this story about anti-abortion extremists could be used to smear the entire Irish anti-abortion movement, by lumping all of them in together with the actions of some truly immoral people. This was three years before the referendum and the debate was so often bitter and ferocious. I thought the Pro Life Campaign or the Life Institute would be put under pressure to distance itself from these tactics and clarify that it didn't support them. It turned out I had dramatically overestimated the Irish anti-abortion groups, and given them way too much credit.

Not a single one of the main groups – Pro Life Campaign, the Life Institute or the Iona Institute – distanced themselves from or criticised the actions of these Catholic anti-abortion extremists. In fact, a lot of their spokespeople eventually just started attacking me instead. I had incorrectly assumed that everyone – whether they believed abortion was right or wrong – could agree that deceiving a woman in order to force her to continue a pregnancy was a terrible thing to do.

What is it about a woman's life that makes it so easy to interfere with? Particularly at such a fateful moment as when she's deciding to be a mother? You would think with the way the Church cherishes and respects motherhood that any Catholic activist would respect the role too much to force someone into it. This is before we even get to how the woman's own choice is erased and dismissed.

A lot of Irish Catholic groups have a ferocity and zeal for stopping abortion that I have never seen applied to social injustices like homelessness or general inequality. Even in a hypothetical world where everyone believed abortion was wrong, why would we rank the sins in utero higher than all of the other terrible things that happen to full-grown people every day – many of which also lead to the loss of human life?

In some respects, the media should share the blame because an outrageous comment that a bishop makes about gay men getting married is always going to get more attention than the Church's position on the housing crisis. It's also only fair to the Church to point out that the last decade featured two intense, historic referendums on both abortion rights and marriage equality. But when I think about the things that were said in TV studios or from the altars ahead of both of those votes, I find it hard to believe that we weren't witnessing the Irish Catholic hierarchy at its most impassioned. I feel that if the Church were as proportionally exercised about homelessness, for example, bishops would be chained to the gates of the Dáil.

My worry is that if I were an alien who landed on earth and tried to learn about the Church from whatever was immediately available, I would think that Catholicism was some sort of exclusive club for people who are inordinately obsessed with other people's sexuality. Catholicism has become an armour for people who are sexist and people who are homophobic, and they've managed to associate the faith so closely with those kinds of views that they've driven a lot of other people away. It's the gospel according to bigots.

I don't think this happened maliciously. Imagine if I was a homophobe. First of all, I would never describe myself as homophobic. (Nobody who is homophobic ever does.) The last decade or so in Ireland would have felt like a direct attack against me. My views have been declared outdated, prejudicial, backwards, hateful and deeply unpopular. This has even been sealed in a national vote. I start to feel like I'm a minority, and I don't think that my views get a fair hearing. I don't want to confront why I feel the way I do. Wouldn't it be much more appealing to rebrand my homophobia as a profound belief? It's not that I'm ignorant, it's actually because I am so devout. That's what Catholicism does for homophobes.

Once you shroud discriminatory views in the respectability of religion, it makes them legitimate. You can demand respect, rather than earn it. And those fighting for equality – like LGBT+ campaigners, for example – are then the ones who become the bigots because they are so intolerant of your religious beliefs.

I've listened to all the arguments about the traditional family, about what the Bible says, about the institution of marriage. My belief is clear: anyone who believes that the institution of marriage is only for straight people is homophobic, regardless of how uncomfortable they are with that label. Trying to deny anyone a right based on their sexuality is bad; pretending it's God's will is much worse.

It cannot be a coincidence that the two groups of people who lose out the most rights-wise from Catholicism – women and LGBT+ people – happen to be two of the groups, alongside people of colour, who have endured the historic discrimination of almost every major institution and industry in the world. The Catholic Church was just as liable to reflect the historic prejudices of society as, say, Irish politics was. But everybody decided that Irish politics was too important not to be reformed and made more equal. Nobody would have said that the historic gender imbalance in the Dáil was a reflection of what the signatories – who were all male – envisioned. Nobody would have said that having almost all male politicians was a profound thing that had to be respected and shouldn't be meddled with through feminism or equality. But that's basically the same argument the Church uses to keep women out. And politics is way, way less important than religion – to me, anyway. If politics had to be reformed, then Catholicism definitely should be.

———— ⚓ ————

Catholicism can be attractive to bigots. I know this because I have had the benefit of reading a lot of unsolicited correspondence from the 'good Catholics' of Ireland for the past few years. I, like many journalists, receive bitter and vicious emails, messages and letters at all hours of the night and day explaining in explicit detail what a terrible person I am. Some of them have joked about violence that may or may not befall me. The anger in them would leave you reeling. Initially I deserved this, in the eyes of the people writing these letters, because I wrote those stories about the rogue agencies that were telling lies to pregnant women. Being anti-abortion is a legitimate view, which should be respected. Being an anti-abortion fundamentalist who thinks women should be deceived into having a baby in the name of religion deserves no respect at all.

Later, the letters from the alleged good Catholics arrived because of stories I did about the lives of people in direct provision. Those people will talk a lot about 'keeping Ireland Catholic'. I've learned that this means keeping Ireland white. If I were a bishop, I would be chilled to my core by the number of racists who have used 'Catholic' as an umbrella label to cover their discriminatory beliefs and I would wonder what it is about the religion that is drawing these people in.

At some point 'Catholic' in Ireland has become synonymous with 'right wing'. When I read commentary from conservative Catholic pressure groups like the Iona Institute, I am confused by how much of it seems to be its members continually railing against things like feminism. And not just pro-choice feminism: very basic equality-for-all feminism. It feels less Catholic and more contrarian. And it feels like people who are spoiling for a culture war rather than legitimately promoting Catholic values. I think they want and need to be a voice in isolation. I think they need to be able to claim a monopoly on representing a minority view. And I think there are much more important and appropriate causes for modern Irish Catholicism to get behind than trying to cling to relevance by replicating US or UK right-wing movements.

The Iona Institute comes up a lot when people talk about Catholicism in Ireland, often in a bad way. It's a think tank that is often relied on to provide the opposing view on a progressive social issue. A lot of people see it as a good example of a Catholic group that is at its most passionate when opposing the rights of others – again, LGBT+ people or women. I would also share this view.

I got to know one of the best-known members of the Iona Institute by accident. I first met Breda O'Brien, the *Irish Times* columnist and Iona Institute member, in a radio studio. We had been brought on to a panel discussion together, presumably in the hope that we would have a big fight with each other live on air. A funny concept of 'balance' is used for these broadcast debates, which seems to be based on the premise that there are really only two kinds of women in the world: the first, a prudish Mary Whitehouse type who has made rejecting feminism an entire personality; the second, an insufferable feminist whose only contribution to the world is seeking out 'problematic' behaviour from the comfort of her own privileged position. Breda and I are easily pigeonholed as the former and the latter, regardless of whether or not that is true.

After we came off air, a researcher thrust a yellow taxi voucher towards me and said, 'You and Breda don't mind sharing a spin back into town, do you?' Well, let me tell you, I did mind. From Breda's face, it seemed like she minded very much as well. The most we knew about each other was what we disagreed on, which was almost everything.

The journey was fine. It turns out we both attended the same secondary school in Dungarvan, but it was under a different name when Breda was there. We had a chat about it, and Breda was dropped off first. When she got out of the car, she turned to me and said something about what a pleasant surprise it had been to have a nice chat with me. (She was being friendly and genuine but I thought it was hilarious.)

When I started to work on going back to the Church, I got in touch with her to ask her a few questions. She seemed totally blasé about my crisis of faith, as if it was the most normal thing in the world or almost as if she'd expected it to happen. She was hugely helpful and very generous with her time when I was doing research. She gave me the names and numbers of a lot of different nuns from back home in Waterford who might be good for me to talk to.

I also really wanted to talk to her about the Iona Institute. We sent a few emails over and back to each other, discussing it. She made an interesting comment one day about how 'orthodox Catholicism is now so countercultural that it is impossible to share in the context of a book interview why we believe what we do unless there is a shared set of cultural understandings'. That made me want to talk to her even more. I had felt embarrassed to tell people that I wanted to be Catholic, so I agreed with her to an extent. I wanted to ask her about that, plus loads of other things. Why was being anti-abortion and against LGBT+ rights such a core, important value to 'orthodox Catholicism'? Would someone like her even want people like me back in the Church? Would she consider people like me a threat to the faith if we came back but put pressure on the Church to reform?

I offered to send her some of my questions in advance in an attempt to persuade her to talk to me. I tried to be as honest as possible and not hide the things I wanted to know, but I think it just pissed her off. One of the questions was: 'Do you think it's possible that the Iona Institute may have turned some people off Catholicism?' Another was: 'How come people in the Iona Institute have written so many columns being critical of the climate change movement, when the Pope has been so clear in advocating for climate justice? Do Christians not have a responsibility to fight against climate change as the ultimate pro-life position?'

She immediately took issue with the climate change question and pointed out that she herself had never been critical of the climate justice movement. I agreed, but said that I was referring to the Iona Institute as a whole. David Quinn, for example, has been critical of Greta Thunberg to the point that I was sometimes worried he had some sort of fixation. Maria Steen, another conservative commentator and member of the Iona Institute, once filled in for Breda's Saturday column in the *Irish Times* with a piece headlined: 'Climate Justice Campaign Resembles a Pagan Cult'.

Breda said she agreed that the plight of asylum seekers should also be prioritised by Catholics, and this is something she herself had written about.

'I'm not involved in the day to day of Iona even though I think it is a vital voice in ensuring diversity in Irish debate. Nor is there a corporate Iona stance on most issues. My views tend to be different from David's on lots of issues but we cooperate on key issues. I don't think I am the right person to talk about this,' she wrote to me.

I tried a couple of times more to persuade her to change her mind, but my last email went unanswered so I decided to leave her alone.

Maybe I'd have more luck with a man of the cloth. The one good thing about a crisis of faith is that it isn't boring. When I wasn't worrying about whether it was right to go back to the Church, I was in anguish over whether or not someone like me would even be welcome. Justine McCarthy had described feeling unwanted or under suspicion when she went to mass. Who wants their pastor to look at them like they're an outsider?

When I think about people in the Church who probably would not want me, I think of Bishop Alphonsus Cullinan. The Bishop of Waterford and Lismore has said a lot of head-line-grabbing things in his time. In 2019 he wrote to his local schools to warn that yoga was 'not of Christian origin' so it was not appropriate to be taught. (I decided that if I got to meet him, he could probably do without hearing how my school – which is in his diocese – had invited a local eccentric lesbian to teach us yoga.)

The main thing I remember him for is an interview he gave after the referendum on the Eighth Amendment where he suggested Catholics who voted Yes would need to go to confession before they could receive communion.

'If people have knowingly and willingly voted Yes, well, then they have to examine their conscience and go before the Lord and say, "Lord, we got this wrong,"' he told WLR FM.

That was the same referendum that galvanised me to want to go back to the Church, precisely because I thought there were Christian reasons for voting Yes. I'm sure the bishop and I both agree on one point: that life begins at conception. I just don't believe that this view, or any Christian view, means anything or holds any value if it is applied cruelly and inflexibly as a black and white rule to something as varied and grey as life. If all Jesus had done was design a set of rules for us to use to judge the actions of others as wrong, regardless of their situation, then he wouldn't have left us with anything of any real worth. This is why abortion is one of the most controversial social issues in the world – because some people find it really difficult. If you believed that abortion was wrong, but you were also uncomfortable with forcing women to travel for a termination, that is precisely the kind of moral quandary you'd really need your faith to help guide you through.

There were people who voted in that referendum, regardless of whether or not they're religious, who thought that their decision – whatever it was – was the only one that was in pursuit of the greater good. But I'm sure that some Catholics who voted No found it hard, and some Catholics who voted Yes found it hard as well. Because it is hard for some people. I think a Catholic who voted Yes had probably done so because of their Christianity, rather than in spite of it. I think it's outrageous to expect a Catholic to atone for making what they believed was the right choice in line with their Christian values. Especially when the only guidance that any of those Catholics could get from the Irish Church's hierarchy was the rigid blanket statement that abortion is always wrong.

I wrote to the bishop and explained that I felt I wanted to come back to the Church, and I told him why I wanted to talk to him. Bishop Cullinan wrote back: 'I would be happy to speak with you. You are a child of God like anyone else and I have to be open to speak to anyone who wishes to speak with me. However, I would like to get a full list of your questions beforehand. That would be of great help and I will be better able to answer your concerns.'

I obliged straight away. My questions were about the Church's record on abuse, whether or not I would be a hypocrite to go back now, if the last two referendums had damaged the relationship between young people and the Church, if he believed that Catholicism was about more than objecting to abortion and marriage equality, if he thought the Church would ever reform, and if he believed the Church should have a role in fighting climate change and racism in modern Ireland. I also wrote what I wanted to ask him about his confession comment:

'I read what you said after the referendum about people who voted Yes needing to go to confession. I believe that life begins at conception, as I was taught growing up, and I don't believe it's reasonable to expect the Church to reform its position on the right to life of the unborn, regardless of what the law is. But I think that on balance, in my opinion, voting Yes was the Catholic thing to do. Regardless of my own view on abortion, I think that some of the wrongs and unintended consequences of the Eighth Amendment were cruel. I know you and many other Catholics don't agree with that, but I guess my worry is if I voted Yes and I don't agree that I should go to confession for that, would someone like me even be wanted in the Church?'

I sent my questions. No response. A month later, I wrote and said I'd be in Waterford that week if the bishop would like to have a chat. The diocesan office said he was out of the country. That was OK, I said, and asked to reschedule for another time: no response. Weeks later, I tried again. Again, I got no response.

I went back and read his original email: 'You are a child of God like anyone else and I have to be open to speak to anyone who wishes to speak with me.' Of course, it's possible that he was just really busy. But I wondered if something in my questions had made him think I wasn't a proper child of God at all. Imagine if I came across as such an anti-Christ that I had accidentally relieved him of whatever bishop code they follow that means they have to be open to talking to you.

Maybe the clergy see feminists and vampires the same way: invite them in at your peril. Either way, I was disappointed.

When I was small, I had a little children's Bible. I think I bought it myself at the Scholastic Book Fair. (That, a book about Geri Halliwell and a starter kit for training to be a spy.) The cover was red and yellow and it had a few Bible stories in it that were all illustrated with cartoons. The first was the one about the lost sheep – one of the most basic and memorable parables about Jesus. The religious leaders had been having a go at Jesus for 'eating with sinners'. In response, he told a story about a shepherd who had ninety-nine sheep but noticed one was missing. The shepherd left the ninety-nine sheep where they were in order to rescue the sheep that had gone 'astray' and bring it back to the flock.

I went back and reread my first email. I wrote: 'I'm hoping to have as many conversations as I can with people in the Church who might be able to help me understand if I should or should not return to the Church.' Not only was I quite clearly a sheep that had gone astray, I was a sheep that was also willing to be complicit in its own rescue mission.

Even if Bishop Cullinan thought I was a dirty awful sinner, didn't he have a mandate to talk to me the way Jesus had eaten with the sinners? Even if Bishop Cullinan spent the whole time telling me I was wrong or trying to change my mind?

Was it not worth trying to bring someone back to the flock – even if he didn't like me, and even if he thought I was wrong? Why didn't he bother to try? Was that not worth intervening for?

Chapter 11

Our fridge had become a monument to adulthood. I had lived in this apartment since I first moved to Dublin at the age of 24. Initially, the poor fridge was rarely burdened with having to do much more than chill leftover takeaway or keep fleeting bottles of white wine below room temperature for their brief tenancy inside. The shelves were sparsely populated save for lonely fruit that had grown fluff, a forgotten teeth-whitening kit or a mysterious block of Parmesan that needed to be carbon-dated. Time passed, our age increased and our tolerance for vinegary wine decreased. My flatmate moved out with her boyfriend, and mine moved in. The shelves of the fridge became radical new frontiers, featuring previously unknown marvels such as: vegetables. And then the fridge took on a new role as a town crier. Invitations arrived. The upcoming unions of our grown-up friends were announced in beautiful calligraphy on embossed paper, pinned to the fridge door under a magnet from Athens. Invitations appeared for weddings in chain hotels, country houses and castles. Marbled paper, wax seals and engraved writing all promised dinner and dancing and champagne. I would stand in front of the fridge, stare down each new arrival, cast a weary glance at my boyfriend and ask, 'Do you think they're doing the Catholic ceremony?'

In my heathen days, I thought a Catholic wedding ceremony was a grand way to ruin a great day. They tend to start a lot earlier and go on a lot longer than other ceremonies. Hair and make-up appointments have to be infuriatingly early in the day so there is time to make the schlep down the country to a satnav-bamboozling parish church. Beautiful young women step out of double-parked cars and immediately obscure their carefully chosen finery in some itchy shawl or appalling scarf to meet the modesty requirements of the church ceremony. Handbags, fascinators and shoes will always match, but the scarf is often a long-forgotten one pulled from the recesses of a coatrack at the last minute. This bit is always an afterthought – nobody is dressing for this part of the day.

Sitting in the pews, it always struck me how mismatched the congregation seems to its surroundings. The familiar church smells, incense and musk, have been masked completely by the stench of aftershave and developing fake tan. We squish into the tiny rows together, trying to accommodate the berth demanded by ornate fascinators, thick suit jackets and puff skirts.

I recall one wedding ceremony where I had worn a beautiful dress with a Bardot neckline, which unfortunately gave me the arm dexterity of a Tyrannosaurus Rex. I had forgotten my ugly modesty scarf, so I adapted by trying to drape my coat over my shoulders, like a carefree Katharine Hepburn. But it was so difficult to keep it there – I looked more like a tiny child clutching a bedsheet to her shoulders while pretending to be a superhero. I spent the whole ceremony trying to stop it from slipping as I struggled to get up and down from a kneeling position with the grace and fluidity of an unanimated mannequin.

The farce of the ceremony is a tribute to secular Ireland. Nobody young knows what the proper prayer responses are, having not been to mass 'since they changed the words'. If there is a millennial in Ireland who is au fait with the changes the Church made to the liturgy in 2011, they have certainly never been sitting in front of me at a wedding ceremony. The chaos of people not knowing when to stand or sit gives the congregation the deranged appearance of the Oompa Loompa dance from *Willy Wonka & the Chocolate Factory*. Sometimes a priest will finish his bit with a flourish, pause for a moment, sigh and then say with resignation: 'You can all stand up now, thanks.' The more weddings I go to, the fewer people seem to be available when the priest asks for any ministers to volunteer to help him give out communion.

Sometimes the priests make me sad. Priests who do weddings are always in performance mode, reeling out pre-prepared jokes about county rivalries and how useless the groom is. I wonder if they feel pressure to entertain us as part of this grubby exchange. It feels transactional: the couple gets to have the tradition of a church wedding, and the Catholic Church gets to enlist another family into the faith, at least on paper.

You can tell who hasn't darkened the door of a church in years by their reaction when it comes to the child-indoctrination part of the vows. 'Are you prepared to accept children lovingly from God and to bring them up according to the law of Christ and his Church?' the priest says. It raised my eyebrows too, the first time I heard it.

'Bit cultish?' I whispered to my boyfriend.

'Bit cultish,' he said.

The priest comes to the afters, sits at the top table, says grace before the meal and usually disappears before the dancing starts. Later, I'll be talking to a bridesmaid in the bathroom and she'll mention how the bride's sister is gay, the priest is homophobic, they all really wanted a humanist ceremony and sure the only reason they did it was to keep the in-laws happy. What a monumental waste of time.

Things changed when I woke up and realised that I both wanted and needed faith. Before I was brave enough to talk to anyone about how I was feeling, I began to secretly hope when the invitations arrived that they'd be for Catholic weddings. I started to both properly listen to and hear what the priest was saying. Artfully smuggled between the cheesy jokes were messages that I found hugely appealing. I heard a priest use his sermon to talk about how precious love is and how it needs loyalty and trust to truly flourish. He framed a marriage as a difficult but worthy project that requires a lot of work from both people – a stark contrast to the manicured sheen of ideal and perfectly formed love that would gloss the rest of the day. These priests were always evangelical about valuing each other over material things. To stand in front of two people who have probably just spent €40,000 on a party and preach against materialism felt pretty radical to me. The way the Church talks about the sacrament of marriage is beautiful. It's extremely unfortunate that it still can't see it's a sacrament that people in same-sex couples deserve as well.

I'd go to these wedding ceremonies and feel like an interloper or a double agent. I'd look forward to the priest's sermon the whole way through, and listen to it with my undivided attention when it finally came. I felt like I was hiding in churches in plain sight, using our friends' joyous days as a cover to sit and listen to a priest.

People like Catholic ceremonies because it's traditional and so grand. I had always assumed that if I got married my wedding would be a humanist one. One of the appeals was efficiency. Once, one of my friends had a humanist ceremony mid-afternoon in a country house. We'd all been drinking in a little bar next to the ceremony room beforehand, and the marriage was so quick someone's Guinness had just about settled by the time we got back. I had nodded appreciatively. 'That's the way to do it,' I thought.

All at once, the scales fell from my eyes. Catholic weddings seemed so much more profound than my impatience had ever let me see them to be. I would watch couples at the top of the chapel and think how awesome it was to see two people stand in front of a monument to God and make an eternal vow. It's a romantic gesture, and a bit gothic as well. Tying yourselves together in law is one thing; binding yourselves together through religion is another. That, I thought, is a vow.

———— ⚜ ————

Despite the bottleneck of friends' engagements that came at the end of my twenties, weddings did not happen every day. I realised I was missing the regular ceremony of mass, something I thought I would never say. I still remember the sense of injustice I felt as a small child, plucked away from the TV on Saturday evening when *Xena: Warrior Princess* was on and being forced to get ready for mass. In my house, four individual children had to be found and bathed and put in their 'good clothes'. We were wrangled still and roughly brushed, wrestled into crisp velvet dresses and frilly socks and stuffed within big coats with fur collars.

St Mary's Church in Touraneena, my parish, was small and cold. You arrived half an hour early to secure a premium seat beside the yellow-painted radiators that ran down each side of the chapel.

Most of the ceremony was a thing to be silently witnessed. I had some small participatory roles: kneel when told, stand when told, shake hands with the neighbours and the postman when told. The slow procession up the aisle at communion was for special bread that the older children were allowed to have (glamorous, aspirational), which I was later told was also Jesus's body reincarnated (spooky, horrifying).

To even be allowed to know about – never mind attend – such a serious, grown-up event seemed like unusual candour from all of our parents. Normally, children are shielded from anything serious enough to be in any way interesting. With mass, parents would blithely disclose that not attending would mean that you would, unfortunately, have to go to hell.

One of my earliest memories as a child was dropping the collection basket at mass. I hadn't been concentrating when my grandmother passed it to me and it slipped through my tiny hands, all of the coins clashing together like a hundred tiny cymbals. The entire congregation, which was also about 90 per cent of all the people I knew on earth at the time, turned to look. I was in a very incriminating position, kneeling in a big pile of money: one-punt pieces and hexagonal coins, ten- and five-punt notes that had been rolled up like tiny cigarettes for maximum discretion. (To be seen or perceived as wanting to be seen making a generous donation to the collection basket must be a mortal sin.) I stared down at the empty wicker basket in my hands, its rich green lining now completely exposed. I felt awful. I'd blown it. I hadn't even started school yet, and I had already secured my place in hell.

Mass was such a serious place that the only way I remember engaging with it as a child was through either fear or boredom – a poor recipe if you're trying to make mass the habit of a lifetime – and by the end of my teenage years I was barely able to endure it at all.

Now, I was at the end of my twenties and yearning for it. I was dying to have that space each week for peace and reflection. I know this is a bit of a cliché for someone my age. To quote the other Madonna: 'we are living in a material world, and I am a material girl'. People my age are forever seeking things that put spirituality above the pursuit of possessions. After the initial thrill of independent adult living has faded and basic material achievements have been won, you see the rest of your life stretch out in front of you and you'd like to make sure it has substance. We want to be conscious and present and aware of the things that matter. And mass is the OG mindfulness.

I'd been thinking about this one day, with very little self-awareness, as I queued for an outrageously overpriced coffee in a painfully trendy place near one of my old offices. I got chatting to a girl I recognised from work. Somehow, the conversation took an odd turn and I ended up telling her about my anxiety about going back to the Church. Initially, she looked at me the way most other people did when I said that: as though I must be joking. Then, she looked pleasantly surprised.

'Well, I'm a Christian, too,' she said.

Once we got back to the office, she sent me a link for the social media account of a Pentecostal church that she goes to in Dublin called St Mark's. It's born-again Christianity. I didn't know much about being born-again Christian, but the preconceptions I had were not positive. I talked to a friend over drinks about it.

'I think they have pretty bad attitudes to LGBT+ people,' I said, with a straight face.

'What, unlike the Catholic Church?' he said.

Fair.

I went back to the social media account. Its bio said it was 'reaching out to bring people home', which sounded pretty good to me, so I kept scrolling.

One thing was for sure, they were serious about their aesthetic. The church's Instagram account looked like it was promoting some obscure music festival for the rich and woke on the west coast of Ireland, rather than weekly mass. There were pictures of beautiful young people in beautiful lighting standing on a stage, holding a microphone and looking lost in song or prayer. Behind them was the set-up for a full band, lit in purple and blue and pink. Most of the pictures had big white letters across them saying things like 'YOU ARE WELCOME HERE' or 'YOU'RE INVITED'.

Maybe I should try it? I clicked through to the website, which detailed the times and location for its three Sunday services – 10 a.m., 11.45 a.m. and 1.30 p.m. My new friend from work told me that most people went to the 11.45 a.m. service ('in case you're hung-over or going before brunch') so I picked that one.

St Mark's is a former Church of Ireland church on Pearse Street in Dublin. I read up on it and discovered it's where Oscar Wilde was baptised in 1854. The website for the National Inventory of Architectural Heritage kindly describes the church as 'austere'. It is extremely plain. I must have walked past it hundreds of times without looking at it twice.

Before I went in on one Sunday morning, I sat outside a coffee shop across the street and watched everybody arrive. The congregation looked more diverse than the audience at any recent event, religious or otherwise, that I had been to. There was a decent age split, but if I had to guess I'd say most of the people there were 40 and under. There were a lot of families. I think only slightly more than half the people were white.

When I entered, I immediately recognised the stage at the top of the chapel from Instagram, set up for a live band and lit from behind in purple and pink hues. About half a dozen exposed bulbs were standing upright on thick black stands dotted across the stage. Very trendy. Behind this stage, I could see the traditional altar from the original church. Two large TV screens stood on either side of the stage, with a bigger one right in the middle above the band. Each screen featured a cosmic-looking background. In the foreground, white cursive numbers were counting down the minutes and seconds until 11.45 a.m. There were about four minutes to go. Mass that started on time would be quite the departure from my experience with the Irish Catholic Church thus far. At least two Christmases in a row, my mother had driven us to a parish about 20 minutes away because word had reached her that they had a priest who always started on time and said a very quick mass. She had calculated that the journey was worth it.

Volunteers were milling around in navy St Mark's T-shirts that read 'it's good to see you' on the back. A number of people shook my hand and told me how welcome I was. As I looked around for someplace to sit, the lights above the audience/congregation dimmed.

There were seats for well over a hundred people on the ground level, with rows and rows of pews on a balcony above us. It was very busy and filling up fast. A young band took their position on the stage.

The instant the countdown clock on the TV screens reached zero, a young man bounded onto the stage, introduced himself as Phil and welcomed us before asking us to stand. He thanked us for our presence, thanked God and departed from the stage just as quickly, as the band started playing song after song after song.

I noticed a pattern. The songs were, first of all, absolute bangers. All of them were melodic, catchy pop songs with big, cinematic choruses and repetitive endings. The lyrics flashed up on the TV screens above, encouraging us to sing along, and most of the people around me obliged.

By the time we were three songs in, quite a few people were openly crying. The band led the crowd into a big, dramatic finish for a gospel pop song. The same two choruses were repeated over and over – with the congregation growing more confident and louder in its singing with every line. The words were:

> Your Name is higher
> Your Name is greater
> All my hope is in You
> Your word unfailing
> Your promise unshaken
> All my hope is in You

The drum beat was now so loud I could feel it reverberating straight through my ribs. The crowd got louder, more evangelical. Looking around, I realised I was the only person who had her hands clasped in the traditional way for prayer. A lot of people were swaying and dancing. Quite a few had their arms outstretched and their palms upturned towards heaven as they yelled out praise.

The singing stopped, but the band kept playing the bridge of the song. Phil appeared on stage again and started talking to us. He told everyone to pray out loud, to ask for whatever it was that they wanted or needed. A cacophony rose up around me, almost drowning out the music. There were too many people talking at once to hear anyone's prayer. All I could pick out every now and then was the same word, whispered over and over again, from different people: 'Jesus … Jesus … Jesus.'

Phil asked us to hold the praise for 'ten seconds more' or 'just five seconds more', the way a personal trainer would count you down if you were doing a particularly awful exercise.

Then there was a slot for 'prayer requests'. Phil told us about members of the Church who were sick or going through a particular difficulty, and asked us to pray for them.

'It's also important to give thanks for prayers that were answered,' he said.

He told us that someone in the congregation had just been granted a visa to stay in Ireland. And, maybe reflecting the age profile of the Church, he added that, after much prayer, a young woman who was a member of the Church had recently, finally, found affordable accommodation in Dublin. This, I thought, was the most compelling evidence yet that religious miracles may be real.

Everyone there seemed able to wear their faith more easily than I could ever imagine doing. I felt embarrassed, but only for myself. When I looked at everyone else, I felt kind of jealous again – the same way I had in that other church, before I cried in front of the priest. The people around me were totally immersed. They were singing these songs with unbridled enthusiasm, as if Christianity was their favourite band.

Despite the preconceptions I had about being born-again Christian, I really wanted to take the Pentecostal Church ceremony at face value. I found some things I agreed with – criticism of legalism in other Churches – and some things that I definitely didn't – an alarming suggestion that hereditary mental-health issues are made up, which almost prompted me to leave.

Over an hour into the service, my attention was starting to drift when a man, Pastor Des, who had taken over from Phil, started talking about 'twisting the scriptures' during his sermon.

Someone had phoned him to complain about an unnamed Church that was twisting the word of God to suit its own agenda. Pastor Des told us that, while he agreed with what this person was saying, he challenged them on how they knew the 'scripture was being twisted'. It turned out the person had just heard someone say it on a YouTube video.

Pastor Des said that the 'the very worst thing you can do' is take what someone is preaching at face value and not investigate it yourself. He gestured towards a pile of Bibles next to the stage. 'If you don't have one, please take one.' I made a beeline for them as soon as the service was over.

A tall man in his early twenties was standing in front of me, brandishing a copy of the New Testament towards his friend. 'Just start with John,' he said. 'Then see how you get on.' I made a mental note to do the same.

I didn't go back to the church again. But I'm glad I heard what Pastor Des had said. I know Catholics love a good rule, but I like the idea of there being some space for personal interpretation of faith. Isn't the meaning of faith too important to get from a third-, fourth-, fifth-hand source? No offence to the Bible, but I think some pretty big boo-boos have already been made when trying to spread the word of God from a second-hand source.

When I was at St Mark's, a girl was sitting in front of me with a hoodie that said 'that would be an ecumenical matter' on the back. When I looked around at the beautiful stage and the cool lighting and the snazzy sound system, I started to think about my own favourite *Father Ted* quote: 'Maybe I like the misery?'

I'm sure that, for me, some of the appeal of Catholic mass is sentimental and nostalgic. I like the austerity of it as well. I like the decadence of Catholic churches, the beauty of the iconography and the reverence for the subjects of the statues and the paintings. I like how the appearance of the churches contrasts with the sincere and muted way we pray in them. It feels respectful and right. I like the cold, stripped-back pews, even the harshness of the knee rests. I like the message and the understated way that it's delivered. I even like the theory behind communion – how that tradition has endured so many years. And I love the symbolism of it as well.

I was pretty sure I wanted to be a Catholic. Now I knew that if I went back to the Church, I wanted to be a Catholic who went to mass every week. All I had to do was work up the nerve to show up.

Chapter 12

'1850,' the deep and unnecessarily provocative man's voice purrs, '715, 815.'

Drums kick in, music picks up and then a familiar voice: 'Hello, good afternoon and you're very welcome tooooo ... *Liveline*.' And then the best bit: when the fiddles go mad.

Liveline gets slagged off sometimes, but I think you'd be hard pressed to find a programme's archive that's a better repository for social change in Ireland. Joe Duffy has fielded calls from an Ireland in conflict with itself over all kinds of change, often offering nothing more than a supportive and non-judgemental 'Gwan, gwan' in response.

Liveline has been an open-source confession box, and it's hosted the micro and macro of social debate. It's also been a bellwether for change. I remember days and days that stretched into weeks and weeks when the programme devoted itself entirely to the experiences of women in maternity hospitals. It came just when the country had started to vindicate reproductive rights and wonder about the frequency in our social history of medical scandals involving women's healthcare.

I've always admired the programme for being a real, democratic leveller. The well known and the anonymous get equal airtime. *Liveline* doesn't have to follow the rules that other news programmes do, where the worth or value of what someone is saying is often proportional to their 'importance'. Sometimes people praise *Liveline* as a way that normal people can talk to the country. But actually, it's Joe Duffy who gets to talk to the country. The country is *Liveline*, and the rest of us get to listen in.

Just after a quarter to two one afternoon, when I was working from home, my WhatsApp groups started to light up like Joe Duffy's proverbial screen. 'Turn on *Liveline*,' 'OMG, *Liveline*.'

Two people had taken issue with an outrageously popular drama, broadcast on RTÉ, that featured frequent and passionate sex scenes. They decided to air their frustrations with Joe Duffy. A caller leading the charge was a man called Tommy Banks, a well-known anti-abortion campaigner who had helped put a very large 'NO' on the side of Ben Bulben in the run-up to the 2018 referendum on the Eighth Amendment.

The show was compared to pornography, it was 'fornication', there was a loose suggestion that current social attitudes to sex in Ireland might have been to blame for the

Covid-19 global pandemic. Sex scenes on RTÉ after the watershed were all but put on trial for every moral failing in modern society.

I listened. I was bristled for outrage, but just felt bemusement. This sort of mad sanctimony used to be the source of heart-stopping stress during the marriage equality and Eighth Amendment referendums. Young people believed, incorrectly, that this was the voice of an electorally significant number of people in Ireland. We were worried that this ethos existed in bigger numbers than we could allow ourselves to think about, and that this stubborn cohort would stand in the way of control of our own lives. Those debates felt so precarious and losable that even the most bizarre and hardline views could cause panic – as though they had a chance of swinging things. There is nothing wrong with having a society that includes people who hold these beliefs, by the way. But at times the rhetoric would suggest that these people *were* Irish society. It turned out they were the louder minority rather than the silent majority, despite what we were told.

But once there are no referendums to lose, any sense of threat that listening to these people could create is neutralised. It's grand! Air your views! Damn fornication on the national airwaves all you like. You could have replaced the Angelus with it, for all I cared. I opened my phone and saw others felt the same. People were quoting the discussion to each other on social media and joking about it. It felt like these curmudgeonly callers were just being humoured.

There was another thrilling shift to the tone of the conversation on *Liveline* that felt very new to me as well. As Tommy made grand pronouncements about the dangers and pressures young women were being exposed to by an over-sexualised culture, some of those listening decided they were well able to speak for themselves.

Young women started calling in. I listened, in awe, to a 19-year-old girl casually declare her right to be an autonomous sexual being on one of the national broadcaster's flagship radio programmes.

A long time ago in Ireland, this would have been the voice of the social pariah. Even in more recent times, we would have listened to teenage girls talk like this but maybe with an eye roll. We would have dismissed this as the view of some cosseted baby feminist, cocooned from the world by a privileged upbringing.

It blew my mind. Young girls who liked to have sex were the normal, reasoned and accepted voices. It was the arch-conservatives who were the abnormal minority, and theirs were the views that were being questioned. When a teenage girl said she had a right to have consensual sex outside of marriage, nobody was saying 'Why?' Often, you can only really appreciate the scale of change retrospectively.

There was also no compulsory respect in this discussion. Nobody was knitting their brows and talking in a consternated fashion about how we needed to force ourselves to respect the beliefs of people who think that sex outside of marriage is morally wrong. It seemed to be cheerfully agreed by the vast majority of us that being up in arms about consensual, joyous sex outside of marriage in this day and age was such an unpopular view that it was verging on an eccentricity.

Unlike in the old days, where he would have been the ringmaster of the circus of acrobatic debate, forever pursuing the elusive state of balance, Joe Duffy sounded more like an indentured servant contractually obliged by RTÉ to sit and listen to anybody at all who could pick up the phone and recall one or two commandments.

'Ah, please,' Joe would say every time the conversation strayed towards more extreme sanctimony. 'Aaaah, come on now.'

Then the programme started to annoy me. Tommy, totally unfazed by the unpopularity of his views, seemed bolstered by his belief that he was on the side of righteous moral Catholicism. He talked about the damage that sex outside marriage does to 'the immortal soul'. He dismissed the views and laws of the State on the age of consent because, he said, the vast majority of people in Ireland describe themselves as Catholic. And as he correctly pointed out, the Ten Commandments forbade fornication.

It is correct that having sex outside of marriage is breaking a commandment. I also don't think it's too controversial to say it is a commandment that the vast majority of Catholics these days do not agree with. I'm not even confident that most clergy agree with it.

Tommy was a caricature of Catholicism. He was also the only person on the programme who was identifying as Catholic. Caller after caller, I waited for another Catholic to weigh in – somebody who didn't agree with Tommy. But nobody did.

'Are you a Catholic?' Tommy asked a man who praised programmes that put a focus on consensual sexual relationships. The man said he wasn't.

'Are you not?' Tommy said, in a self-assured way. 'Well, OK.' He went on to dismiss another woman as a 'lapsed Catholic' for taking a different view to him.

I was becoming really annoyed – to the point that, for one chilling moment, I almost called *Liveline* myself. The programme, by now, had descended beyond debate into pure entertainment. Tommy was an isolated figure, a lone voice for the most popular religion in Ireland; but certainly not, to my mind, someone who was in any way representative of modern Irish Catholicism.

I thought this was ridiculous. I thought it was frustrating. I also thought it was embarrassing. And so, it finally clicked. I must be Catholic.

Finally! I had realised that I was a real Catholic through the medium of the most appropriate emotion of all: shame! I was scarlet listening to Tommy because I thought he was making Catholics look silly and backwards, and I only cared about that because I was finally truly and fully identifying as Catholic myself.

When I'd thought about Catholicism up until this point, it was as an outsider who was wondering if I should or would ever get back in. A year earlier, I probably would have scoffed at Tommy and moved on. But now, it bothered me that the portrayal of modern Irish Catholicism on *Liveline* had been so ridiculous.

I had been hoping for a long time that something like this would happen. It was all well and good to get lost in the intellectual arguments for and against religion, but since that day I'd cried in front of the priest, I had learned the value of trusting my feelings. I have a *grá* for the spiritual parts of religion, the ones that verge on paranormal activity, so I was very confident that somehow, someday I would just know that I was Catholic again.

Some part of me was even expecting a sign. I had taken to randomly walking into churches when I passed them. If I was early for an interview with someone, or had a bit of free time ahead of a press conference, I would amble into whatever church happened to be near. Churches in the middle of the day were quickly becoming some of my favourite places, particularly the ones in Dublin. The serenity in them is hard to find anywhere else in town. I wanted to visit these churches to say a quick prayer anyway, but I sometimes wondered if one day I'd walk into one and feel something click. I was kneeling and saying proper prayers and all that, but I still felt like I wasn't fully there yet. I didn't yet feel like 'a Catholic'.

There's a comfort to wandering into churches in different parishes that isn't totally dissimilar to the strange reassurance of wandering into a McDonald's anywhere in the world and it being familiar. The sense of peace in churches always felt the same, and I liked that.

Something I had missed, without realising, when I was unreligious was the ease of prayer when you're in a church – particularly in the still and quiet hours outside of mass. Private prayer at home is really important, and I don't think the connection to God is any less, but there is something special about how easy it is to fall into deep prayer in a church – like when you're exhausted and slip into sleep with almost no effort.

There is a beautiful church on Merrion Road in Dublin. It sits across the road from St Vincent's hospital, on a little intersection of science and faith. My consultant works at St Vincent's, and I always made sure I made time to visit the church before my appointments.

There's a weight to the silence in that church, which must have heard many muted pleas for all kinds of help from the people crossing the road from the hospital over the years. I bet people have asked for all kinds of miracles in there. I bet some of them got them.

I was sitting in the church one day, after saying a prayer, and I started to let my mind wander. I wondered what God thought of me and my fraught attempts to come back to the Church. I wondered if He was pissed off about how long it was taking, or if He thought I was being incredibly self-indulgent about the whole affair.

I looked around me, self-consciously, and then looked straight ahead at the altar. I tried to give it a bit of an understanding nod. 'You would tell me if I was wrong about all this, wouldn't you?' I asked in my head.

Innocuous silence. Well, what did I expect – some sort of review? Was I looking for a sign? Imagine if I did get a sign. I started to overthink it then and wondered what would happen if I experienced an apparition. In the spirit of good Christian honesty, I should disclose that I briefly considered that I might pretend it never happened. Could you imagine the hassle? I read that even St Thérèse had nuns bitching about her when she came forward about the Virgin Mary healing her. If you claimed to see an apparition in 2020 you'd get nothing but grief. And probably a twelve-part podcast based on your life, presented by an introspective American host who wonders aloud what made you such a compelling scammer. I wonder if there have been any modern apparitions that we don't know about for this reason, because the person just walked away, whistling, back to their quiet, uncontroversial life. Maybe thinking this way is precisely why I would never be chosen for an apparition.

Anyway, I had no apparitions in empty daytime churches. But I did start to feel more and more Catholic. And with surprisingly little effort on my part, it started to have a weird power over my life.

—⟶ ⚜ ⟵—

A long time ago I employed the services of a personal trainer. I was shocked into action one night when I jokingly flexed my arm for my boyfriend, and he laughed loudly and impolitely at the sight of my 'muscles'. He even pinched the space where a normal person's muscle would be, incredulous that I could even open doors, hold a pen et cetera with such paltry upper-arm strength. I decided to pursue a personal fitness project. My devotion to this project can probably be measured by the brevity of the relationship between me and my personal trainer.

I went on a spending spree for the snazziest, pinkest gym gear I could find and merrily went to meet my new physical tormentor. After that first early morning session, I had stumbled out of the gym in a state of cardiac and emotional distress. I staggered up the flight of stairs to my flat, my thighs screaming. I was in a state of physical pain that I believed was much more than could be healthy.

Pinballing between all of the furniture in my living room before finally collapsing on the couch, a strangled cry escaped my lips.

'What,' I gasped, '*is* this?'

My boyfriend gazed back at me, dispassionately, over a spoon loaded with his breakfast cereal.

'Is it supposed to hurt this much?' I whined, full of self-sympathy.

'That's how you know it's working,' he said. 'It has to hurt if anything is going to change.'

I do recall, from my brief time as a healthy person, that once you make the conscious decision to be good about food and exercise it is much harder to be bad. It also, infuriatingly, starts to *feel* pretty good – vindicating everything that any dose with a decent Instagram following and an ambassador role for a fitness brand has ever said.

Choosing to skip a session or eat poorly made me feel physically bad and mentally bad. The strength of this guilt was so powerful that I once showed up for a training session the morning after the national journalism awards and had to be sent home due to the crushing stink of booze and the fact that I was evidently still intoxicated.

Guilt gets a very bad rap, but it has its uses. As the urge to be religious again started to creep back into my life, the guilt for my sins started to come with it. And I realise now that one of the wonders of faith is that it perseveres long after any sane personal trainer would have abandoned all hope of a change in behaviour. Even when I kept sinning, over and over again, I felt a pang of guilt every time – so the aspiration to stop this kind of behaviour never seemed to fade.

I'll give you an example. I don't know what metric St Peter uses to calculate the badness of each sin. A lot of sins aren't included in the Ten Commandments. Who decides if an embezzler is worse than a money launderer, for example? But if the severity of sins is based on the frequency with which they are committed, then one of my greatest sins has to be bitching. I bitch with the freedom of someone who must surely think that she is perfect herself. But I don't! I just love bitching.

I must have spent hours of my life tearing strips off people, without once feeling so much as the feeble stirring of my conscience. After I started to pursue religion, this changed. I was sitting on the couch one night, carrying out the efficient and forensic character assassination of a woman I used to work with, punctuating each offensive remark with a theatrical swill of my depleting wine glass. I finished my tirade and breathed a sigh of relief. Letting off that kind of steam was usually a therapeutic experience, as if the flaws of others were some sort of personal burden that I alone had to shoulder. But only moments later, the bad feeling crept in. *That wasn't very Christian of me, was it?*

I am not spending any time coiffing my locks for the imminent application of a halo just because I've finally started to feel bad about being bad. Feeling guilty about doing bad things was a new sensation, but not one that caused a radical change in behaviour. However, the good thing about guilt is that it doesn't seem to give up on you when it clearly sees that you're a helpless gossip. So while I haven't stopped bitching by any means, I have started to feel bad about it. The religion thing is working.

Gluttony, pride, envy: I was starting to feel bad about all of it. Another 'sin' that I hadn't expected to feel differently about was the way I use the internet. I've always found it strange how people still draw a distinction between the internet and so-called 'real life'. People work on the internet, people fall in love on the internet. We decide what to eat, sleep and drink based on what we see on the internet. If that does not yet qualify it as part of 'real life' then I don't know what ever will.

Invigorated by my freshly discovered Catholicism, my conscience started to needle me about some of my behaviour online. Fortunately or unfortunately, social networks like Twitter have now become part of the public sphere and public life. Some political stories even break on Twitter. If you're a journalist, like me, a presence on and participation in Twitter has become a job requirement.

I've spent a lot of time on Twitter over the past few years. Some of my best stories even came from tips that people sent me in private messages on Twitter. I've also made some really lovely friends on it. (Yes, 'real-life' friends. Meeting strangers from the internet is normal now.)

I said before how I've gotten a lot of abuse on Twitter – mainly from anti-abortion extremists. And when I say extremists, I mean extremists. I don't think it would be enlightening or useful to spend too much time going into the specific details of what that abuse has included over the years. Just trust me that, at times, it was devastating. There were days when abusive tweets people sent me had dispro-portionate control over me, my life and my happiness. One day after my new employer had announced on Twitter that

I'd gotten a new job, I lay flat on the couch, holding the phone directly over my face, scrolling numbly through the kind and congratulatory tweets. I was just waiting, waiting, waiting to feel the sting of a cruel and abusive one. Reading the nice tweets, I could feel nothing. Finding a nasty one, my body would flush hot and cold and my stomach would twist. A unique feeling of shame and anger and sadness would take over my whole body. I'd feel the low hum of depression and an element of self-loathing. I'd wait, and then go looking for another nasty tweet. It was as close as I imagine I've gotten to genuine self-harm. This was all very unhealthy, and it was frustrating and difficult for the people I love to have to watch.

But that was not the source of my conscientious problem with social media. As you can see, if you're fortunate enough to not know first-hand, Twitter can be a very nasty place. People can be abrasive, and any time you get a notification, there is a reasonable chance that it's from someone attacking you. This is a deranged environment for humans to spend hours of their days existing in, and it had an effect on how I interacted with people.

What I hate the most about online abuse is the way it makes me behave in response. It's not in a very Christian way. When someone is horrible to you, your instinct is to believe or maybe even prove that you don't deserve it. When I see someone saying truly horrible things about me, my immediate urge is to get someone else to reassure me that

that person is wrong. I see lots of other people doing the same thing.

So the temptation, which I have often given in to, is to retweet the original abusive tweet and draw your followers' attention to it. What often happens then is an instantaneous stream of messages asking me if I'm OK, reassuring me that the abusive person is horrible and maybe even mocking the original premise of their criticism. But what undoubtedly happens is that the people who follow me will take it upon themselves to abuse the person who sent the nasty tweet in the first place. It will be well-meaning and defensive, but it will absolutely be abuse – the assumption being that anyone who abuses someone deserves to be abused themselves.

Then there are times when I engage in a row myself. Because I've spent too much time on a forum where being attacked is normal, sometimes I can be too quick on the trigger and too likely to snap back at anybody who tweets anything marginally critical at me. I've been more likely to exacerbate or even start a futile row with a random stranger, which eats up minutes and hours of my precious life, than I have been to simply put the phone down. It's a petty, unpleasant and embarrassing way to behave. And it creates an avatar of me online who seems much crueller and snarkier than I am in real life. I have tried almost everything to stop engaging with this over the years. I've fleetingly locked myself out of the app, changing my password on myself. I deleted the app. The only thing that ever worked was …

Catholicism. The guilt associated with throwing barbs at people – even people who are not very nice – was the only thing powerful enough to stop me. I consciously pivot to extreme normcore, tweeting about pleasant walks and moderately difficult recipes a lot instead. Certain stories – on sexual violence, abortion and the rights of asylum seekers – inevitably spark more personal, anonymous abuse. I block instantly. There's an interesting phenomenon on social media that reminds me of Bible parables about judgement. With so many truly appalling and hateful sentiments online, it's become alluring to use them as a way to mark ourselves out as better. So when someone says something shitty, there's an insatiable urge to highlight how you don't agree with it just to make yourself seem like a better person by contrast. The worst sentiments can spread the fastest online by the sheer volume of people sharing them just to prove they disagree with them. It's a way to mark yourself out as good or shame others for being bad – or both. It took a long while for me to understand the futility of letting other people's bad behaviour draw out bad behaviour in me. So I've also tried to stop initiating conflict by smugly pointing out how I disagree with a bad person's comment.

I know I'm skirting close to becoming one of those eccentric evangelists who likes to sit backwards on a chair and ask young people if they've 'recently accepted a Friend Request from Our Lord and Saviour, Jesus Christ?' The internet is an important element of my life, and I largely love it. But this change in behaviour prompted by Catholicism is probably the one that has had the largest day-to-day effect on me. I can't put into words how many hours of pure misery it has spared me.

My little online fracas have dropped off dramatically. When a nasty message does get through, I seem to have a stronger will to mute it or ignore it, or at least think before I respond. The guilt worked.

I'm not sure how much faith I have in myself to always be good or to always do the right thing. The inflexible structure of a religion that will in some ways help me to hold myself to account is very appealing. It's like having a Fitbit for your soul.

The guilt helps me to feel like my spirituality has an objective. Spirituality is super popular at the moment with people my age, but religion isn't. I think there are enough writers in the world already trying to divine the exact motivations and concerns of 'the millennials' through broad, sweeping statements in newspaper columns. I don't need to add to that. What I will say is that I believe that as a much more visible generation, based on how much we declare and publish about ourselves on the internet, our search for meaning as we move into our thirties and beyond has been easier to spot as a trend.

I've seen waves of my friendship groups turn to tarot cards, the occult and something that seems describable only as 'extreme horoscoping'. There is zero shame around anything that speculates what else there may be to life and what unseen forces could be already deciding our paths for us.

We also have a real desire to be good. Look at the climate justice movement. Look at veganism. Genuinely laudable pursuits like these – in a small number of cases – can tip over into a public display of moralistic worth. If and when that happens, it does so in a way that is not unlike how some people wear their religion in a pious way. In some cases, virtuous projects can even be used to mask or excuse objectively bad behaviour. I've seen examples of people with eating disorders dressing up their condition as a moralistic diet like veganism or 'clean eating' – one that you can exhibit online and be actively rewarded for with public praise.

So we want to be good, and we are open to spiritual beliefs. I wonder if there's a parallel universe where the Catholic Church didn't completely fuck up, and where Irish people my age have become the most devout generation yet, after cling-ing to religion through decades of national and global chaos.

But back in this universe, there's little chance of that happening. And catering to nomad believers my age is a lucrative business. You can sell peace of mind. Snake-oil salesmen have been drawn to the world of mindfulness and wellness, after those who were genuine and well intentioned discovered that it's a field in which a reasonable amount of money can be made. This is another reason why the aus-terity of Catholicism is appealing to me. The words 'luxury mindfulness retreat' are an oxymoron.

I understand that it's not rare for someone my age to go looking for deeper meaning in the world. Maybe my sudden yearning for Catholicism is a misplaced example of the consequences of getting older and more in touch with my own morality, but I don't believe that it is. I know myself that the depth of belief I have in God is very real, and I don't feel an especially strong pressure to need to prove that to anyone else.

And what makes me feel better about it is the guilt. Even if I died and discovered I was incorrect about God and religion, I wouldn't be embarrassed because I would know that believing had helped me to lead a better life. The guilt is like a security blanket, which lets me know that my pursuit of religion will have been worthwhile regardless of what comes after. At the very least, even if I was wrong about it all, it will have made me nicer to people.

Chapter 13

There is a deep and intellectual argument against religion that points out that it defeats itself if the only reason people are drawn to it is for reward. It's a fair point. It would undermine my entire belief that people are solely and fundamentally good if the only reason that millions of people were drawn towards Catholicism was as some sort of queue-jump to the Good Place after they die. I know I'm still learning the Catholic ropes, and I don't want to unravel too much progress at this point, but I do have another confession to make: I don't really believe in heaven.

I believe in an afterlife of some description, and I believe that God and all our deceased loved ones are 'there', if you can use such futile physical earth words to try to describe such a place. I suppose this is somewhat close to the traditional understanding of 'heaven'. I just don't really believe the part about people having to meet and exceed a goodness threshold to get in. And I don't believe in the hell part at all. I don't think there is any such place as hell. Even if there were, I can't imagine God having the vengeance to put anybody in it.

My uninformed, mortal guess is that the classic ideas of heaven and hell were inventions of necessity to try to mitigate the unreliability of humans. People are fundamentally good, most of the time, but they definitely require assistance. Guilt works for me. Maybe other people are more carrot than stick. If what I believe to be the fictitious concept of heaven and hell helps to guide people towards the greater good in the end, then I think that's just fine.

Personally, my belief that everyone – even the most apparently warped, sick and cruel person – has some fundamental good in them leads me to believe that all souls get into 'heaven'. My understanding of the thing that Jesus wants from humans is just for us to try to be as nice as possible to each other while we are on earth, to improve the collective existence for everyone. I think that's an admirable enough project on its own that God wouldn't have felt the need to justify with a prize at the end. So I'm not in it for that. I'm pretty sure there is something there after we die. But even if I died and my soul instantly evaporated into the abyss, I'd have gotten everything I wanted from religion while on earth.

I like Catholicism because it helps me try to be a better person. I think that Catholicism could also help to create a better society. A lot of Irish people will, for good reason, never feel comfortable going back to the Catholic Church. They might see it as an oppressive or even evil force. I don't want to make those people nervous when I talk about Catholicism contributing to societal good. The Catholic Church shouldn't ever return to the position it had in Irish society, where it was part of the powerful elite and started to rot from the inside out. I also don't believe that Catholicism should be given a particularly special status ahead of or above other faiths in Ireland, just because of its history. All I am saying is that it still remains one of the largest religions in the State, and I think there is potential for it to be a positive force for change. I'm talking about a version of the Catholic Church that is an outside advocate or activist, not a Church that is restored to an undeserving place as part of the national establishment.

I know that someone could have gone through the same considerations I did about the Church's position on women, LGBT+ people and its handling of abuse, and easily come out the other side deciding to walk away from the Catholic Church completely. I think that would be fair. While some people may not understand it, I've come out of it looking in the other direction. Let me try to explain.

I feel about religion the same way I feel about politics. I love politics, but I loathe Politics. I worked briefly as a political reporter and was largely based in Leinster House for a lot of my working week.

Leinster House reminded me of the horcruxes from *Harry Potter*, which would slowly turn people who wore them into much worse versions of themselves. I felt like simply being in the building made me a worse version of myself, and the same seemed to apply to other people as well. Everything is fast and chilly and a bit acerbic in there.

It's strange that a place founded on such a romantic and aspirational concept as democracy could be so bitter and cold. It'd be rare enough that you'd stop for a chat in the corridor of Leinster House and end up saying anything positive about anyone. A good day for one person inevitably meant a bad day for someone else. You had to wear an armour of cynicism at all times. That gets very heavy and very boring.

There were moments when you realised what a privilege it was to be in there, when you saw the democratic process contract and contort itself to force through an objectively good result. But those moments were rare. Or rather, I should say, it was rare that those moments were noticed. Many tropes about politics and people in Leinster House are total bullshit. Most politicians aren't malicious, for example. But the big broad machine of politics that people have to fit themselves into can be just as depressing and inflexible as it's sometimes portrayed.

Once you see the uglier side of politics, it's easy to lose heart in the virtues of democracy. And in fairness to Irish politics, Leinster House is hardly a unique, or even the worst, example of the grubbier side of politics.

All over the world, democracy has failed people disastrously and repeatedly. If you wanted to, you could make a compelling case for abandoning the system completely. It would be easy to sit and list all of its faults, to put it on trial and declare it a failure. You could try, and possibly succeed, in arguing that the bad things democracy caused have cancelled out the good things that it did.

Democracy and religion are both examples of commendable human projects designed to improve people's lives. Both of them, in broad terms, are based on the noble aspiration to make the world a better and fairer place. But both of them have, unfortunately, been attractive to or even served some of the worst traits of humanity.

We often talk about dramatic changes in Irish politics, but some of the people who advocated for the things that happened in recent years died before they could see them happen. Change can be achingly slow in coming about. And for those who feel disenfranchised by the people who govern, the prospect of trying to change who they are can sometimes feel futile. But still, we all vote.

I'm glad that even at times when it seemed beyond reform, people put pressure on Irish politics to be better. It is too important to do anything else. You wouldn't bother criticising and trying to change a system if you didn't respect it. People will keep participating in a system that they respect and value, even when it appears to be doing nothing for them, even when it's the antithesis of their own values. The remote prospect of change makes it worth participating in at an individual level.

That's why I'm going back to Catholicism. I think it's too important to me to abandon it.

I am not going back in there demanding that it change just to suit me. In all honesty, there's a reasonable chance that I'll have died before the Church changes its position on LGBT+ people or women. But it will change eventually, in this century or the next. I'm sure of it.

When I first started trying to go back to religion, I thought the best I could hope for was a way to balance the fundamental conflict between my own values and the more controversial views of the Catholic Church. That was before I was radicalised by priests.

I think that a notable proportion of the Irish clergy and laity want change. I don't know how many, but it's possible they could even be one of these 'silent majorities' we've heard so much about over the years. Others will say that I'm a feminist brat, who has swept in after spending a wet week back in the Church and now expects an institution that is thousands of years old to change just to suit me and my left-wing beliefs. It's a fair criticism. I would point out that I don't expect the Church to change all of the policies it has that I don't agree with. I think that abortion is too nuanced an issue to be navigated by a view as hardline as the Church's. However, I would never expect the Catholic Church to reform its views on the right to life because I understand that that is a very profound, key teaching. I do believe, as I've said previously, that the Church should look again at how that pro-life belief manifests itself. Why is the Church only interested in getting involved and having a view after conception? Wouldn't all of society be better off if the Church used whatever power and influence it had to try to eliminate abortion on socioeconomic grounds completely?

As for its views on LGBT+ issues and women: as a good Catholic, I am supposed to believe that the Pope is God's spokesperson on earth and everything he says is the will of God. I just cannot ignore my conscience and pretend I think that homophobia and sexism represent the will of God, and that it isn't possible that humans have misused the faith to serve its own prejudices. I think the Church has succeeded in creating a climate where the possibility of that having happened can't even be discussed.

Doesn't it strike you as strange how many priests are only willing to talk about that off the record? Don't you think it's weird how an organisation as big as the Irish Catholic Church could be so sensitive to the slightest, most obvious criticism? Isn't it upsetting that clergy, who have devoted decades of their lives to that vocation, still don't feel like they're allowed to talk? Isn't it devastating that they would rather leave?

I was afraid for a long time to talk about any of this sort of stuff out loud. I thought I'd be dismissed for my poor understanding of the Old Testament or quizzed on the intricacies of Catholic theology. I thought that I had not earned the right to have an opinion on any of this because I hadn't been saying the rosary every night. I thought that people would just say I was an à la carte Catholic, someone who dipped in and out of the scriptures when it suited.

I was baptised and raised Catholic and I believe in God. Any one of those things should be enough to prove that I also have a stake in the future of the Irish Catholic Church. You don't need qualifications to be part of this conversation. Not only do people like me deserve to be part of the debate, I think we're the only people who will actually start it. The Church is never going to change on its own.

All of this began because I was asking if going back to the Church was the right thing to do. I incorrectly assumed that I would be supporting the institutional Church, when I didn't understand that it was just something I could use to support myself and my faith. Like that priest said: I don't like the postman, but I'm still going to take the post. Nobody can count my presence in a pew on a Sunday as another vote for homophobic or sexist policies. The routine and community of weekly mass is important to me, but mass is not a political rally. While you wouldn't know it from the outside perception of the Church, there is a lot more to Catholicism than its controversial and conservative social policies. I would not be the first person to go to mass and take what I need from it, while knowing there are parts of the Church that I don't agree with. So I don't feel any guilt about going back to the Church. However, I do feel some guilt *ahead* of going back to the Church.

The vast majority of the criticism aimed at the Catholic Church in Ireland over the last number of decades has been, I think, justified. But I do understand now that, in the past,

I was sometimes too quick to assume that the motivations of the Catholic Church were always nefarious. Like a lot of people, I treated anything Catholic with a degree of suspicion. There are huge swathes of Irish public life where the Catholic Church should not have control – health and education, for example. But there are other parts of public life where it might suit to at least hear a Catholic perspective – I'll get to those bits in a little while.

When I was a teenager, I went through a stereotypically petulant phase of rejecting religion and indulging in some mortifyingly fervent atheism – it was all grand and harmless. Many people who go through a similar experience grow out of it and grow to appreciate the value and comfort of religion to others – even if it's not for them.

Ireland has had it hard. Our whole national identity was interwoven with Catholicism from the very start. The religious freedom to be Catholic was hard won. When we became an independent nation, we became a Catholic country. For such a young sovereign state, our history has been blemished by a lot of episodes known collectively as 'dark chapters'. Those were also interwoven with Catholicism.

At times when the country was trying to move forward, the Church was often trying to keep us back. The Irish Catholic Church's very recent history is defined by opposition to progress. That is all before you even consider the damage caused by clerical child sex abuse.

So I think Ireland has had a harder time separating out

the theoretical good of religion from the established bad overseen by the institutional Church. The Church was the establishment here for a long time, so it's sometimes treated the same way a political party is when it betrays people. A lot of people can't or won't forget.

I think that's why it's tougher for some of us to even contemplate going back to religion. I understand people who feel that way. For a long time I was someone who felt that way. Speaking only for myself, I realise now that I often failed to separate the institution from the faith. And in dismissing one, I also dismissed the other. I'm sorry about that. Sometimes I was actually involved in a row about culture when I thought I was in a row about religion. Those are two very different things.

I think I'm very lucky to live in the Ireland that I live in now. It's an exciting time to be Irish. There have been changes in this country that we've been privileged to live through.

Over the last decade, the whole country has spoken about things that it never spoke about before. There has also been deep national introspection about where the State went wrong during its first hundred years. The Church has rarely come out of those conversations well.

When things have been covered up for so long, you need to give people a chance to deal with them in their own time. Sometimes I get a sense of frustration from those in the Church, a feeling that we're lingering on its mistakes for too long and refusing to move on. I don't think the Irish Catholic

Church will ever be allowed to move on from its mistakes. I don't think it should be, either. Forgiveness is a Catholic virtue, but for the individual. Societies that help write histories shouldn't be in the business of forgiving and forgetting. What the Church did should be recorded and remembered forever. But you can have a different conversation that lets the Church have its own future, independent from the State, without completely erasing the unforgivable aspects of its past.

For me, religion is personal but it is also political. All of the values of social justice that I think are most important for the future are 100 per cent in line with Catholic values. Catholicism does not have a monopoly on these values, and I'm aware that other religions are available. But, to me, Catholicism feels as permanent as my national identity. It's not about shopping around and finding the easiest religion and changing to that one. I think I, and anyone else who wants to, should have a right to remain in the religion I was born into and be allowed to hope for reasonable reform and improvement.

As I said before, when people talk about Ireland as 'a Catholic country' it's meant in the pejorative sense. Diversity and secularism are important. I don't want to 'restore' Catholicism to the position of unchallengeable power that it had in the past. So I don't want Ireland to be a Catholic country, but I do want it to be a country which includes Catholicism. The way things are at the moment, I'm not sure if that can be guaranteed. Churches are closing, priests are retiring without being replaced and those who remain are expected to take on more parishes. Beyond the unsustainability of it, I think it is also possible for the Irish Catholic Church to become a much smaller and sadder organisation in my lifetime.

I think it's natural that, given Ireland started in a position where the power and influence of the Church was so extreme, the pendulum has swung back to the other extreme, where a minority of people see Catholicism as something which needs to be completely expunged from society.

The political debates around the baptism barrier and sex-education reform often rightly demand that Catholic influence is totally removed from schools, which makes sense. As I mentioned before, I think it's dangerous for a school's religious ethos to be able to stand in the way of a modern, inclusive and comprehensive sex-education curriculum that challenges rather than conduces homophobia. I completely agree with the theory of having schools with a religious ethos, but any argument in favour of them based on the premise of religious freedom is undermined by the fact that many non-religious parents in Ireland have no freedom and have to choose a Catholic school.

I really wish that the Catholic Church would make an effort to appear as passionate about other social issues, so that it could start making a case for its inclusion in other debates. It is still the most popular religion in the State, and it could have a valuable contribution to make around housing and asylum issues. But there is a possibility that Catholic involvement in any political issue could still be seen as too loaded for some. The problem is that Catholicism is so closely associated with misdeeds that it's hard to recognise it for doing any good at all.

Chapter 14

A few years ago, I wrote a story that took on a life of its own and became much bigger than its component parts. It became a microcosm for cultural rows over social change in Ireland and a split between the Church and the State. It was about a new national maternity hospital (NMH).

At the time of writing, the NMH is based in Holles Street, where it has been since 1894. It's too small and it's too old. For ages, there has been talk of a new hospital that would be built on the site of another adult hospital – in line with best international practice. In 2013 it was decided that it would make sense to build this new hospital on the site of St Vincent's hospital in Dublin. St Vincent's, at the time, was owned by a religious order called the Sisters of Charity.

About a dozen hospitals in Ireland are, like St Vincent's, owned by the Irish Catholic Church. After the foundation of the State, the Irish Catholic Church was majorly involved in helping to fund and run healthcare services in Ireland.

All over the world, the Catholic Church is still the biggest non-government provider of healthcare services. Providing healthcare has always been a core part of the faith and it made sense that this kind of assistance was needed for a country like Ireland, which was just finding its feet as a sovereign state.

So today, about twelve voluntary hospitals are run with public funding but are owned by religious congregations. There have also been previous cases in Ireland where hospitals owned by secular organisations had an archbishop sitting on their board. This has caused problems over the years, as more and more things that became normal healthcare procedures clashed with the teachings of the Catholic Church. For example, in 2005 it emerged that the Mater hospital in Dublin had deferred a lung cancer drug trial because it would have required women on the trial to take contraceptives. The drug could have been damaging to an unborn child, but the use of contraception was seen as being in conflict with the Catholic ethos of the hospital.

This is just the way things have always been in Ireland. It wasn't until the NMH scandal that the relationship between public healthcare and private Catholic groups was scrutinised under such intense focus

In 2013 Holles Street and St Vincent's hospital began to plan how the governance of the new NMH would work. Holles Street, the existing NMH, wanted to have their own independent board for the new hospital. Like the existing

NMH, this was planned to have an obstetrician as master of the hospital. But St Vincent's wanted the new maternity hospital and the existing adult hospital to be governed by the same board. The idea of a Catholic hospital being responsible for the governance of a maternity hospital caused quite a bit of consternation. When it comes to the kind of healthcare procedures a Catholic hospital is likely to object to, a lot of them relate to obstetrics and gynaecology.

In 2016 the government tried to appoint an intermediary between St Vincent's and Holles Street to see if the row could be sorted. An agreement was reached, but this turned out to be only the beginning of the palaver.

In March 2017 I got a tip-off that the agreement would allow the new NMH, which was going to be built with public money, to be owned by the Sisters of Charity because it was built on their land. It took me the best part of a week to get the story into the paper, mainly because I was so sure that I must have had it wrong that I checked the story with the HSE about three times.

Often the most shocking stories are not the ones about really brazen, malicious decisions, but short-sighted or ill-thought-out ones. The Sisters of Charity, at that point, still owed €3 million to a State redress scheme for child abuse. To gift them such a major piece of national infrastructure, particularly one that related to women's health, seemed totally inappropriate. But the HSE was pretty po-faced about it and gave me a fairly unapologetic statement.

Even within my own newsroom, some people were blasé about the plan for the hospital and suggested it might not even be a story. This was, after all, the way that things had always been done. News is, by its name, supposed to be about new developments.

The story ran and, at first, nothing happened. I shrugged it off. Maybe most people thought the plan for the hospital was pretty innocuous after all. Within a few weeks, a larger newspaper than mine ran the story again. It exploded.

Plenty of stories over the years have referenced the possible influence of Catholicism on Irish healthcare. A story like the one about the Mater hospital rejecting a drug trial because of its Catholic ethos had all the components required to cause national uproar and raise major questions about the separation of Church and State. But that was 2005; the NMH story was 2017. And timing was everything.

There's a really cheesy line from a John Green novel about how you fall in love the same way you fall asleep: 'slowly, and then all at once'. Ireland seemed to renounce the Church the same way: resentment slowly creeping in as the secrets crept out, before Irish society seemed to consciously take a big step back from the Church in 2017.

Just weeks before the NMH controversy emerged, one of the darkest and most disturbing stories emerged from the ground in Galway and the eyes of the world fell on it.

'Significant' human remains were discovered at the site of a mass grave in a former mother-and-baby home in Tuam.

In 2015 the Irish government had set up a commission to investigate the standards and treatment of women and children in these homes, which were run by religious orders, between the early 1920s and the late 1990s. The remains were estimated to be of unborn babies from around 35 weeks' gestation to two- and three-year-old children. Headlines ran around the world about this 'chamber of horrors'. Enda Kenny, who was the taoiseach at the time, said that Tuam was 'a social and cultural sepulchre'.

All of the media coverage tended to use the same photograph. It was what looked initially like a very small, unremarkable site covered in grass. This was the site of the former home. A stone wall ran around it. In the far right corner, you could make out the blue and white of a Marian shrine. Outside the site, a shiny, new-looking black plaque paid tribute to the loving memory of 'those buried here'. A small black metal gate sat next to it with a white cross in the middle. How different the white cross seemed to the horrified spectators of this story to how it would have seemed back in the 1920s. Maybe it looked honourable then or even distinguished. Now, it looked menacing.

Once again, Ireland was horrified by the Church. I found it remarkable that we hadn't yet become immune to these horrendous stories. The version of Ireland that was broadcast around the world was a particularly dark and sad one. It was utterly depressing to watch.

And the NMH story was sandwiched between this shock from our past and a surprise about our future. Weeks later, about a hundred people would assemble in the humble function room of a hotel and set in motion a chain of events that would eventually lead to a free, safe and legal abortion law for the first time in the history of the State.

On 23 April 2017 I was sitting at the back of the Grand Hotel in Malahide, watching the results of the citizens assembly roll in. Ninety-nine citizens had been selected to consider the Eighth Amendment and Ireland's ban on abortion. The politicians had basically taken an issue that had been haunting them for decades and let the people sort it out. I'd spent weeks following the assembly. They went through abortion rights from legal, medical and ethical perspectives. It had been forensic and tough, but one thing that it was not was overly heated. Once the same polarising spokespeople had had the debate taken off them, normal Irish people had proven to be well able to parse the issue themselves.

The committee voted to repeal the Eighth Amendment, indicating a referendum would be likely to take place. This wasn't a surprise. Then they moved on to vote for the new abortion law they believed should replace the constitutional ban on abortion.

I was sitting at a small table at the back, which was adorned with a thick white tablecloth, perched on uncomfortable chair that had probably spent other evenings decorated with a bow for a wedding or a debs. A couple of journalists were sitting around me but it had not, so far, been a major media event.

With absolutely zero fanfare, the committee announced, through the underwhelming medium of a crappy projection onto a screen, that the majority of its members had voted for free access to abortion 'with no restriction as to reason'. A free, safe and legal abortion law.

I looked up at the screen and down at my page in confusion. I checked again. It still said that 64 per cent of the assembly had backed free access to abortion. Alison O'Connor, the columnist and journalist, was beside me. I could see her mouth moving as she quickly calculated the same jaw-dropping percentages. She raised her eyebrows and shrugged her shoulders in a kind of 'I don't get it either' way.

While it is the law now, free access to abortion up to 12 weeks was politically inconceivable then. Legal abortion services were only ever discussed in the context of women who had a sad enough story to deserve them. 'Rape, incest and fatal foetal abnormalities' was the mantra used in place of 'free, safe and legal'. It reminded me of the coarse stipulations that reality TV shows use. There had to be some sort of narrative arc. You had to earn the abortion by suffering first.

I turned and looked behind me. I could see Linda Kavanagh from the Abortion Rights Campaign, who looked in such a state of shock you would have assumed that the assembly had gone against her. Behind her was Cora Sherlock, from the Pro Life Campaign, her face totally blank and her hands resting, motionless, in her lap.

Little cups clinked against saucers; the assembly members pushed back their chairs and stood up and stretched. It was as if they'd done nothing at all. I was rushing to write up a story for the next day's paper. Hunched against the wall in a corridor of the hotel near the function room, I couldn't even believe the words I was writing. It was monumental. And it directly led to the new law introduced in 2019, following the successful repeal of the Eighth Amendment.

So 2017 felt like a tipping point. A lot of things were changing. The NMH story broke right in the middle of a social tinderbox, when Irish people seemed ready to rail against the Church.

The NMH story only ever became as big as it did because of the reaction from the public – in particular, from women. Women immediately rallied and organised. A petition against the State's plans to gift the hospital to the religious order attracted more than 100,000 signatures. There were protests. TDs were inundated with correspondence from outraged constituents. The government came under major pressure.

I've always thought that Irish people have a great sense of social justice. While I know not everybody here is Catholic anymore, it strikes me as quite a Christian trait for a country to have. When I think about the Irish public, I imagine the archives from the original *Late Late Show*: people who are quiet and attentive most of the time, but righteous and loud when it's called for.

The sense I got at the time was that people didn't want to be in this three-legged race of a country where the Catholic Church was always tied to the State. The desire for a different model for a new maternity hospital was strong and, I believe, justified. At this point, plenty of parents were enduring the glacial pace at which the Church was divesting from schools. I imagined people felt that if the Church was entangled with the new NMH from the start, it would be very difficult to unravel. And even if the Sisters of Charity weren't a religious organisation, why should any private group benefit from the ownership of a public hospital built with public money?

But something else was happening with that story. It felt like a kind of final straw – the intensity and the heat of the criticism of the plan for the NMH seemed to be about much more than just the hospital itself. A row that was effectively over the ownership of an asset was twisted very quickly into a tale of good versus evil, where the State was on one side and the Church was on the other. While I agree completely that the State was wrong to plan to gift the hospital to the Church, aspects of the discussion made me a little uncomfortable.

First of all, there was some misinformation about 'the nuns'. 'I am not giving any hospital to the nuns,' Simon Harris, the former health minister, said darkly in the Dáil chamber one day, reassuring TDs that 'the nuns have said they are leaving'. One could imagine 'the nuns' as malevolent witches of the night who had latched onto the maternity hospital, like a bat infestation, and had to be exorcised from the building site with a sprinkling of secular water. The phrase 'the nuns' in the modern Irish political context, understandably, does not conjure an image of a benevolent group of kindly-faced matrons.

The story became muddled very quickly, and there were some inaccurate suggestions that 'the nuns' would not only own, but actually run the hospital. The language was hyperbolic, and conjured images of nuns patrolling the corridors, rosary beads in hand, on their way to set up a cloaked wing for unmarried mothers. One source close to the project asked me, in exasperation, 'if the people really thought they were going to build a Magdalene laundry in the basement of a new maternity hospital'.

There were legitimate concerns that a maternity hospital owned by a Catholic organisation could restrict access to healthcare services like IVF. Or abortion, which was becoming a conceivable Irish legal healthcare service. Dr Peter Boylan quite rightly pointed out that no Catholic hospital in the world allowed abortion, so why would the Sisters of Charity make an exception for Ireland? Any attempts to rebut this by the order were a bit watery and opaque, so concern understandably grew. In the absence of proper clarification, it was suggested terminations would definitely be banned outright at the hospital – and I could see no evidence for that. There were certainly valid reasons for concern about the ownership of the hospital, but the Church was not going to run it.

I would rather not be in a position where we had to trust the word of the Irish Catholic Church with regard to women's healthcare. But I found it hard to imagine a modern maternity hospital, which would be run by obstetric staff who had likely already been working at Holles Street, not allowing abortion after it had been a legal health service for years already. There certainly are small maternity hospitals in parts of the country where anti-abortion obstetricians have effectively been able to stop abortion services since they were legalised in 2019 by conscientiously objecting. If you only have three obstetricians and they all conscientiously object, then your hospital is not going to be able to provide terminations. And some maternity hospitals are more pro-choice than others. But senior staff at Holles Street were some of the most prominent medical experts supporting and calling for the repeal of the Eighth Amendment. The idea of our most senior obstetricians, working at one of the biggest maternity hospitals in the State, being told by an order of nuns that they could not perform abortions was inconceivable to me. Even if that were the case, and the hospital's owners tried to ban abortions, the ensuing uproar would surely resolve the issue very quickly.

The debate grew heated, and there was a lot of distrust on both sides. Even those who were traditionally pro-choice were growing exasperated with the controversy. Some even claimed that those advocating for the Sisters of Charity to be removed completely from the hospital were slowing down the entire project and causing women to lose out in the long run. Dr Rhona Mahony, the former master of Holles Street, was reported in the *Sunday Times* as telling a friend that feminists were going to ruin the new maternity hospital for women.

The story started to morph into something else entirely. At times the political commentary around the story read like a Brothers Grimm-style tale about one rogue order of nuns determined to keep their vice-like grip on the control of women's healthcare. The Sisters of Charity seemed to get pissed off about this as well. At the height of the row, the St Vincent's Healthcare Group (which is owned by the order) put out a statement saying it was reviewing the status of the project. This was perceived immediately by some as a threat to the future of the hospital – the Order would deny this. St Vincent's blamed 'controversy and misinformation' and specifically mentioned remarks that Simon Harris had made. At the time, I asked a PR company working for the group if the statement meant that the hospital wouldn't go ahead, as some had suggested. A PR emailed me back and said, 'It says what it says.'

The Sisters of Charity had been involved in healthcare services in Ireland for over 180 years. I understand why some would have been annoyed if they got the impression that that record was effectively being erased. The Sisters of Charity was founded by Mary Aikenhead, who also founded St Vincent's hospital in 1834 as a hospital for the sick poor.

It was Catholic social justice that motivated her to create the hospital, not status or influence.

But the initial Catholic involvement in healthcare appeared to be rewritten during the NMH debacle as a power grab rather than an act of charity. I don't believe any information from or about the Sisters of Charity supported this theory.

In May 2017 the Sisters of Charity announced that it was fully stepping back from healthcare and relinquishing its control of St Vincent's Healthcare Group. As with everything in the NMH palaver, this was met with deep suspicion. The Sisters said that ownership of the group would be transferred to a new company, but it did mention maintaining the values of Mary Aikenhead. This was immediately read or misread to mean a sneaky Catholic ethos would remain in the new group. Sources pointed out that Mary Aikenhead's work had actually predated the Catholic Church deciding it was against abortion.

The Sisters of Charity had been planning to move away from healthcare anyway but had effectively been pushed out much sooner because of the NMH scandal. I believe that the result – having a hospital that is not owned by a religious order – is the right one but I do appreciate that, at times, the Sisters of Charity were taking the heat for a lot more than the core NMH issue. This was a row that became about much more than a hospital. It was a row about Church and State, which became Church vs State.

I've asked the Sisters of Charity to talk to me about this, but they said no. An offer was made, through their PR agency, for me to send some questions in writing, which I did. Unfortunately, I didn't get a response.

The Sisters of Charity only ever communicated through a PR agency, which made clarity and nuance a lot harder. Even now, years on from the initial controversy, any article about the whole palaver will almost certainly see you get a terse email from a slick PR the next day on behalf of the Sisters. These emails are often seeking niggly corrections and clarifications for tiny inaccuracies, both real and imagined.

However, the Sisters' case wasn't helped by their colleagues in the Irish Catholic Church. Some ill-advised pronouncements from other senior clerics definitely made things worse. Kevin Doran, the Bishop of Elphin, gave an interview with Justine McCarthy where he suggested that the new hospital would have to obey the rules of the Church. Reports that the Sisters of Charity would have to obtain permission from the Vatican before they could transfer ownership of St Vincent's were downplayed. But years later it emerged that that was precisely what had to happen. The Vatican did give permission for the land to be transferred in 2020, despite some pleas from Irish clerics for it to refuse to do so because the new hospital would inevitably be performing terminations. I've asked the Holy See some questions about this – is it an unusual decision for the Vatican to take? Why did it agree to transfer the lands knowing that terminations would take place on the hospital grounds? They did not respond.

In response to the row, the Irish Catholic bishops drafted a new code of ethics for Catholic hospitals, which it published in 2018 following the referendum on the Eighth Amendment. It was unambiguous. It banned abortion, contraception including emergency contraception, some transgender health-care and most assisted human reproduction in Catholic hospitals. In the few cases where assisted reproduction was allowed, it was not to include unmarried mothers or same-sex couples. I personally didn't read this as others did: like a manifesto for the Irish Catholic Church keeping its hand in healthcare for another generation. With the depleting number of orders involved in hospitals and the inevitable reduction in religious-owned hospitals, I read it more as an ideological protest in favour of what the Church would see as its right to keep Catholic hospitals Catholic. (If the Church wants to have its own hospitals, I have no ideological opposition to that. But it shouldn't be running them with public money.)

This code of ethics came after the country had voted to legalise abortion. Politicians had been clear. Catholic hospitals would have to perform legal healthcare procedures, including abortion.

But the code of ethics for Catholic hospitals advocated going against the law if it was in conflict with the Church's teaching. So, in theory, a hospital would refuse to offer a woman an abortion even if she was legally entitled to one. This is based on the idea that the Church would be saving a life, and this justifies extreme action. I wonder where this audacious zeal for social justice is when large properties are lying vacant during a homelessness crisis, for example. If breaking the law is justified in the name of the Catholic good, I'd like to see this guerrilla Catholicism happen in areas other than women's reproductive healthcare.

All of this, including the code of ethics, felt less about what would or would not happen in a Catholic hospital and more about a culture war between the Church and the State. It felt like the Church was just flexing and shadow-boxing. There had also been threats before the 2013 Protection of Life During Pregnancy Act, which legalised abortion when the woman's life was at risk, that hospitals simply would not perform terminations. There was no evidence, that I could find, that hospitals were regularly refusing terminations on this ground, though it is worth adding that the number of abortions carried out for this reason each year was very small.

The tone and rhetoric of some of the outcry around the time of the NMH scandal seemed to suggest that the whole affair was evidence of some residual deference to or fear of the Catholic Church on the part of the State. It was suggested that this deal was the product of the State being in bed with the Catholic Church, unable to sever its ties from it. I find that hard to believe.

Politicians are exactly that: politicians. It was obviously politically popular at the time to advocate for the clear separation of Church and State – particularly in healthcare. If you see something suspicious – like how long it takes for the State to remove religious influence from schools or hospitals – I always find it useful to consider there's been a fuck-up before assuming there's been a conspiracy. Separating Church and State is complicated and protracted and frustratingly slow, but I have zero reason to believe that the failure to successfully do so up until now is because the government feels reverential towards the Irish Catholic Church. The way some in the Church talk, they think the government is openly out to get them! At the time of the NMH story, there was talk of different ways that the State could make sure abortion was available in 'our hospitals', meaning any hospital run with public money, even those owned by a religious order.

For example, right in the middle of the controversy in 2017 the Irish government announced a review into the role of voluntary hospitals in Irish healthcare – including religious hospitals. The aim was to examine the relationship and, based on what politicians were saying privately at the time, untangle it. But the results of the report didn't really suit the popular narrative. It pointed out that if Catholic hospitals were refusing to perform certain procedures and the State threatened to defund them as a result, we'd all be worse off. 'In reality, the State would not be in a position to replace the extensive range of services provided by Catholic organisations,' the report said.

There was some masterful spin to keep that inconvenient fact off the front pages. Journalists were fed little details in advance about calls to remove holy statues from hospital wards. After some more questions, the government finally admitted that it didn't actually accept that part of the report, but by this point the news agenda had moved on.

That's the way the Irish health service exists at the moment. Whether the public thinks it's right or wrong, it can't actually exist without Catholic hospitals. So while everyone is in favour of untangling and unravelling the Church from Ireland's public healthcare service – including many in the Church itself – this needs to be done gradually over a long time with mutual respect and cooperation. It probably isn't something that could be done, say, in the time a person spends as health minister. Eventually, it is something that will serve both sides. Despite the rhetoric around the NMH scandal, I can't see much evidence of many Catholic orders actively wanting to remain involved in healthcare in modern Ireland. The Sisters of Charity had been planning to step back anyway. It's estimated that the twelve Catholic hospitals we have at the moment will eventually be whittled down to four as a result of religious bodies withdrawing from healthcare provision. This is also partly down to the decreasing number of priests and nuns that we have in Ireland.

The lesson I learned is that political discussions about Catholicism are extremely polarising. There is no room for nuance in any political row that involves the Catholic Church. Personally, I think the new national maternity should be owned by the State, but if that's not possible, an independent secular organisation is probably the second-best option ahead of a religious order.

But the NMH dispute showed me very clearly and up close that when you involve the word 'Catholic' in a row, the Catholic side can be easily and quickly villainised to extremes that don't serve anybody. When the Catholic Church feels it is being disproportionately attacked, it can lash out, making it appear belligerent and doing nothing but exacerbating the distrust that people hold for it.

I feel uncomfortable when valid criticism of the Church veers into arguing for Catholicism to be completely banished from Irish society. There is no way that Catholicism should control schools or hospitals, and it has taken too long to separate out religious ethos and influence from such key national infrastructure. But I don't want us to throw the baby out with the bathwater.

If there is going to be another generation of Catholicism in Ireland, the Church needs to find new ground to work on. Nobody is in any doubt about its opposition to marriage equality and abortion. But every time there's an election, is it really a good use of time to have a bishop calling for Catholics not to vote for pro-choice politicians? It's the same topics over and over and over.

There are other issues in Ireland. There are bigger issues in Ireland. And the just and humanitarian side of the argument around these issues is often aligned with core Catholic values. To mangle a phrase, get the ovaries out of your rosaries. There are other things that we need the Church to save its prayers for.

Chapter 15

Despite the popular belief that journalists are bred in test tubes in D4 as part of the Dublin Media Elite, I spent my childhood on a farm.

There were dogs, cats, birds, sheep, cows, mink, rabbits, foxes and insects of all kinds on my grandparents' farm, next to the house I grew up in. They were all treated with varying degrees of hospitality, depending on their place in the delicate little ecosystem.

I vividly remember cycling through a laneway covered in a canopy of trees, parallel to one of the main fields, when I saw the dead rabbit in a snare in front of me. These snares were one of a number of things the adults warned us to stay away from on farms, along with slurry pits and rat poison. Farms are great places for children to push their personal safety to its absolute limits. There's a clear threshold between safe and dangerous, and skirting the line helps you respect it. A rope was attached to the roof of a barn, which we used to climb up to, hold onto, swing on and jump off, landing in the bags and bags of sheep's wool below. This was OK, as was climbing on hay bales. So anything that was deemed not OK was usually almost certainly lethal.

I was afraid of the snares. Up until then, when I was seven years old, I had managed to never see the consequences of one. The rabbit looked almost perfect: its glassy eye was open and it was staring at me. I stared back for a long time, feeling sick. Eventually, I turned my purple Raleigh bike around and started to walk it home.

Killing any animal was wrong. It was a sin. No matter how many times the facts of life on a farm were explained to me, no matter how many times I was reassured it was a quick and relatively painless way for the rabbits to go, I was always upset about it.

I remember being given a rifle to hold a couple of years later, and feeling the heavy wood of it rest against my shoulder. I imagined it kicking back against my small bones when it was fired. I hated the feel of it. The rifles on the farm were for shooting foxes. I loved foxes as well, and I felt like guns were a cop-out way of killing from a distance.

I couldn't even hurt a fly. I was too afraid. I'd been taught clearly that all creatures were God's creations. St Francis of Assisi was my favourite saint, and one who I imagined more like the protagonist of a Disney film. All the pictures I saw of him when I was small were of a man absolutely adorned in birds and animals. I imagined him wearing all these little creatures like a living, moving, breathing coat.

The farm taught me a lot about the worth and value of the natural world. It was literally putting food on the table. It also formed a lifelong *grá* in me for the Irish countryside.

In the decades since I was small, we've learned a lot more about the natural world and its increasingly precarious state. I've stood in Merrion Square and listened to articulate, amazing teenage girls talk about imagining a world where there is no beautiful Irish countryside. The beauty of nature is a very galvanising force.

I was raised on a perfect cocktail of ruralism and Catholicism, which made me extremely sympathetic to the climate justice movement. But climate justice has, unfortunately, often been framed as an existential threat to farming in a way that has way too often polarised farmers against climate activists and vice versa. The argument has become too muddled and sometimes been portrayed as the hobby horse of rich, anti-rural suburbanites. It's a shame.

But Catholicism is different. Opposing climate change is the ultimate pro-life policy.

Since he took over, Pope Francis has been very strong on the issue. (Pope Francis was a source of hope for many who wanted the Church to reform, but a lot of the people I spoke to mentioned feeling disappointed that not much had changed since 2013.) He has criticised Donald Trump's attitude to the Paris agreement; he has urged huge oil multinationals to keep it in the ground; he has even advocated for taking radical individual action and boycotting certain products that harm the climate.

In 2015 the Pope published a 165-page document that set out the Catholic case for climate action. It's called 'Laudato si', and it's the second encyclical letter from Pope Francis. It's pretty dense. I don't mind disclosing I did not get through it. Two years later, the Pope gave it to Donald Trump as a 'gift' following a meeting between the two leaders. It was widely seen as a pointed move on the part of His Holiness.

The Christian position on climate change is very clear. Climate change exacerbates the refugee crisis; it worsens hunger and poverty. It is disproportionately caused by the richest countries and disproportionately affects the poorest. It's unfair. Climate justice is social justice. Social justice is a Catholic value. And all of that comes before you even consider the moral and theological arguments for protecting a planet that the Church believes is God's handiwork.

Remember how Justin McAleese explained to me how influential it would be if the Church changed its position on sex education about LGBT+ people? It would have the power to directly change the policy in schools attended by millions of children across the world. I felt very hopeful about the Pope's position on climate change for a similar reason. While the power to change the Church's sex education on LGBT+ people rests with those running Catholic schools, there is a degree of individual power with climate change. A strong message to over a billion Catholics from the Pope should be a radicalising force.

But from what I can find out, five years on from the Pope publishing the encyclical, the impact has been underwhelming, if not a bit dispiriting. In 2017 research by the International Journal of Cognitive Science on US Catholics found that they were more likely to be led by their political beliefs on climate change than their religious ones. And because climate change is seen as an issue popular with those on the left, conservative Catholics were less likely to be influenced by what the Pope was saying. People appeared to be looking at their religious values through the prism of their personal political beliefs. (Like me, right?)

Research by Yale in 2015 suggested that Catholics who already didn't trust the Pope as a reliable source of information on climate change were even more polarised and trusted the Pope even less after 'Laudato si'. The problem seems to be that a lot of the things the Pope calls for in order to appropriately respond to climate change seem to criticise economic growth at any cost. This is precisely the same reason that some of the young school strikers in Ireland have been dismissed as too left wing: because they've condemned Fine Gael governments for pushing economic growth above and beyond just transition and responsible climate-change measures.

Well, on the bright side, if conservative Catholics are allowed to pick and choose what Church teachings they follow based on their political beliefs, then there shouldn't be a problem with Catholics like me choosing to ignore the teachings that don't align with my personal values. Though

I would point out that, of the policies I want to ignore and those right-wing Catholics want to ignore, only one will definitely lead to the destruction of the planet.

I can't find any studies about the impact of the Pope's message about climate change on Irish Catholics, but a similar, if not worse, problem has emerged.

The most prominent lay 'spokespeople' for Catholicism in Ireland all come from the same political leaning – they're all more to the right of the political spectrum than left or centre. This means that the national newspaper columns these people have are more likely to represent right-wing policies than all-Catholic policies.

I had hoped to talk to Breda O'Brien about it and had included a question on the topic in my email to her. The Iona Institute has several critics of the climate-change movement among its number, and they regularly use their columns to say so. (Like the one that called the movement a 'pagan cult'.)

The Irish Catholic bishops do regularly mention the message of protecting and looking after our earth, but the most attention-grabbing lines from the New Year's pastoral messages are often condemning the types of social change that came the year before. The word 'unborn' is likely to feature quite prominently, for example. Again, the main focus is still largely on issues relating to sex.

It seems like Ireland has less diversity in its mainstream lay Catholic voices, which makes Catholic climate justice activism seem pretty sparse, if it even exists here at all. For example,

I was able to find an Irish Catholic nun who works with Extinction Rebellion in the UK but I couldn't find any prominent Catholics in the Irish branch of the same organisation.

Maybe if we had left-wing Catholic voices in Irish media who were as prominent as the right-wing ones, the faith wouldn't appear as deeply unappealing as it does to so many. There is more to Catholicism than anti-abortion and homophobic policies. If cultural Catholicism in Ireland had a greater focus on other social issues, it would probably benefit all of us in the long run.

During the last general election, I was stuffed into a clothing rail inside a charity shop as I watched a man berate Leo Varadkar. We were in Dundrum, the affluent Dublin suburb, and the man had shaken the Taoiseach's hand but then relatively politely started tearing strips off him for his government's climate policy. When you're a journalist on the campaign trail, your main job is to collect the most entertaining and colourful criticisms hurled at politicians, so I was listening in. This man put his hand on his little girl's head and explained to the Taoiseach that the government wasn't doing enough on climate action for the next generation.

Days later I was standing beside the Taoiseach with my notebook out in Tyrrellspass, County Westmeath, when another man eviscerated him for doing too much on climate change. This man was a farmer, who claimed that Varadkar's government was full of out-of-touch elites who were going to decimate rural Ireland through its climate-change policies. It's a lazy stereotype to say that rich people in Dublin care about the climate and poorer people in more rural areas don't. However, perceptions are powerful. If the perception is that climate change is something that only rich people can afford to care about, with no regard for the impact on people in rural Ireland, then it is going to be difficult to get anyone who believes that to take climate change seriously. Climate change is the most lethal threat that the planet faces, and also one that has a disproportionate impact on the poorest in society. You don't need polished politicians to lead on this issue. You need priests. There's a stronger chance of me being ordained than of the Irish Catholic Church appearing as left-wing out-of-touch liberal elites any time soon.

I think that all of society would benefit from the Irish Catholic Church being as passionate about climate change as it is about sexuality issues. While it's nice to think about the Church taking up the mantle solely for the sake of the greater good, there would be plenty in it for the institution itself. To me, the institutional Church feels largely irrelevant and stale and kind of dark. Climate change is the biggest issue of a generation, and it appears to me to be the most obvious place where the Church could maintain some social relevance in the future.

The Irish Catholic Church has been so liberated now that it's lost almost all of its power. It's much easier to understand the plight of people who are left out by 'the establishment' once you yourself are not part of it. The Church is perfectly primed now to be agitating more strongly than ever before as an outsider. The Church should be a thorn in the government's side. And not just during referendums.

The Church has a ready-made – albeit depleting – network of clergy who have access and influence in parts of Ireland where politicians and journalists may have little to no sway. No serious social change has ever happened in Ireland without meeting people where they are. Priests should be meeting them in the pews. I have no doubt there are priests doing great work promoting climate justice in their own parishes already off their own bat, which we don't know about. But again, I wish we could see climate justice preached with the zeal and frequency with which the perceived ills of abortion are denounced from the pulpit.

I think it would also be hugely beneficial for people who aren't religious, or even explicitly anti-Catholic, to see that kind of social justice Catholicism on a grand scale. Seeing bishops who are more exercised about climate change would never bring those people back to the Church, but it might reassure them that there is still a place – though not a special or exceptional one – for the Church in Irish society.

The climate-justice movement claims that much of Ireland's failure to act properly on climate change is because economic interests get in the way. Regardless of how left-wing or unappealing it might sound to conservative Catholics, a cursory reading of Jesus Christ's teachings would leave a person in little doubt that the man was no fan of capitalism. While I wouldn't expect to see bishops in a state of anarchic revolt, there may be no harm in deploying the tried and tested tactic of public shaming against a government that keeps putting the economy before the earth. When Ireland is letting private companies import fracked gas, I would like to hear the Church denouncing it before I hear it from Hollywood actors – which is what happens now.

The climate justice movement should be reaching out to the Irish Catholic Church and asking it for help. It wouldn't be particularly unusual or unprecedented. In 2019, anti-direct-provision protests started to explode across Ireland. This was for two reasons: the first was anger from small communities who weren't consulted before direct-provision centres were opened and the second was racism.

Direct provision has been Ireland's 'temporary' solution for managing and accommodating asylum seekers for decades now. It is constantly beleaguered by controversy and scathing criticism from human rights groups and NGOs. Major and persistent calls are being made for it to be abolished and replaced with a humane and human-rights-compliant system.

At the moment, it's at capacity. And because of the housing crisis, even people who are granted asylum can't move on from direct provision because they have nowhere else to live. The State has started using temporary emergency accommodation like B&Bs and hotels to accommodate asylum seekers, but it has also needed to open more direct-provision centres.

These centres can hold hundreds of people, and because of the controversy of the system, the State's modus operandi for opening new centres in tiny Irish towns is to just do it and not let local people find out about it until it's too late. The theory among some politicians is that if people knew in advance, objections would come in from every councillor and TD within miles.

This method has, obviously, sparked some disquiet where these centres have open. When people started to protest against the centres, racists smelled an opportunity and started trying to either whip up more opposition to the centres or capitalise on the non-racist objections that already existed. This is how bad direct provision is: the poor standards and failings of direct provision are so well known that the human rights arguments against the system started to be co-opted and misused by racists. Direct provision is so bad that even racists don't mind saying so. And there was a natural media focus on the racist aspects to the protests. This coloured the demonstrations and led to the people involved in the protests to feel offended and insulted by what they felt was the media painting them all as racist. This increased polarisation. In the midst of all of this, asylum seekers were being moved into towns where they could clearly see large protests against their arrival. It is not a situation conducive to the warmest *céad míle fáilte*, is it?

Not that it should make a difference to the standard of help which people get, but it's worth pointing out that a lot of the asylum seekers in direct provision are Christian. Priests in parishes across Ireland are often doing great work, quietly, as pastors in direct-provision centres. But it can vary from community to community. A priest told me that, in one parish, the very people who were up doing the first reading on Sunday were protesting against accommodating asylum seekers on Tuesday. There have also been cases where a bishop has written a pastoral letter calling for people to be welcomed and a priest in a parish where there are protests has decided not to read it out.

Either way, the local access and influence that the Church has was spotted by the government. Before the end of the year, Charlie Flanagan, the justice minister, had asked the Irish Catholic Church if it could help promote a welcoming attitude towards asylum seekers.

Isn't that a great idea? I think, even beyond that, the Church should also be helping to advocate for either the fundamental reform or abolition of direct provision entirely.

Direct provision is a dream for racists who don't want any asylum seekers in Ireland, full stop, because the system offers accommodation and food to those who are in it. It's therefore easy for xenophobes to say that asylum seekers should be grateful to have anything at all, we have enough of our own problems and we should be housing Irish homeless people first.

It's not just the poor standards in some direct-provision centres, but the interminable waits. It can take years to have your asylum application processed. That is insane. I've read dozens and dozens of inspection reports from direct-provision centres and you can see the flaws in black and white. But the worst things about direct provision are intangible, and not easily recorded in a report. Your life is on pause. You feel and become institutionalised. You're segregated from the rest of Irish society most of the time. Many direct-provision centres are in isolated, remote settings. Your sense of self-worth depletes quickly. You are known only as an 'asylum seeker'. Things that the rest of us take for granted – falling in love, getting married, having children, progressing professionally – are all delayed or maybe lost completely in those years where your life is suspended. This is on top of God only knows what kind of misery or misfortune these people are fleeing from in the first place.

The online abuse targeting those who advocate for change in direct provision or even journalists who write about it is increasing exponentially. The accounts of these trolls tend to have a lot in common. The first is the tricolour emoji and grand pronouncements of patriotism. The second is the frequent use of fake news or racist propaganda stolen from white supremacist groups in the US. The third is the word 'Catholic'. If the Catholic Church wants a culture war, there is one on the internet ready and waiting for it. Plenty of people are misappropriating and misusing the religion in the name of racist and anti-asylum causes. They see Catholicism as countercultural, a thing being oppressed or silenced by the State. Again, Catholicism is being twisted into an instrument to be used in a culture war rather than recognised and promoted as a religion that is about kindness.

———— ✠ ————

The biggest social and political issue in Ireland for a long time has been the housing crisis. Many of the services that have had to step in to help where the State has failed have been run by Catholic organisations. One of the most notable is the Peter McVerry Trust, which was founded by Fr McVerry.

I visited him to have a chat about social change and the Church. When I arrived, he was in a small office above the homeless youth café that the trust runs on Dublin's northside.

'Do you mind the dog?' he said, gesturing towards the floor. A green and navy sleeping bag was stuffed underneath his small desk. A small Jack Russell called Tiny was snuggled inside. I was about to reach down to her, cooing, when Fr McVerry cut across me.

'Don't pet her,' he said. 'She snaps.'

Tiny used to belong to a homeless man who had rescued her from a shelter. But the man was later diagnosed with cancer, and he gave her to Fr McVerry to look after. She now follows the housing campaigner everywhere. If you google pictures of Fr McVerry, you can often see Tiny standing beside him on stage at a housing rally, next to him on a couch at the trust or scooped up in his arms in a picture taken for an interview.

As we left the office, one of the men sitting outside Fr McVerry's office made the same mistake that I almost did and reached down to pet Tiny. With the reflexes of a fighter pilot, she turned, snarled and snapped at his retreating hand.

Fr McVerry led me into another small room – which looked like it was set up for consultations with service users – and Tiny followed us. She sat at the door, vigilant. Tiny is obviously a very nervous, defensive little dog.

When Fr McVerry was growing up, he believed in a specific type of Catholicism.

'I grew up believing, or being told, that God was a God of the law,' Fr McVerry said. 'That God had laid down all these laws, they were reaffirmed by the Church, interpreted by the Church, and you had to obey them. And your relationship with God depended on how you obeyed those laws. Having come to work with homeless people, I totally changed my understanding.'

He paused and corrected himself. 'No, they totally changed my understanding.'

Fr McVerry would talk to homeless people about their beliefs, and they would tell him that they hoped God wasn't real. 'A young homeless man said to me, "The thought that there might be a God depresses me." And I'm used to people telling me that they don't believe in God, but this went a little bit further. I came to understand what he was trying to say,' Fr McVerry said. 'He felt he was a bad person. He had broken all the laws, and more beside. He felt that God was looking down and saying to him, "There's a bad person. I couldn't love that person." And if he ever died and went to meet Him, God would tell him to get away from Him.'

Fr McVerry explained that he knew this homeless man well. He had grown up in a 'horrific' home with a lot of violence, sexual abuse and neglect. Fr McVerry said he started to understand the anger and the alienation that the man felt. 'I thought that if there is a God, this man must have a special place in God's heart because of all of the abuse that he has suffered as an innocent child. And yet, he was telling me the very thought there might be a God depressed him. And so I moved away from a God of the law to believe in a God of compassion.'

Fr McVerry's new view of the Church was that everyone within the Church should lead happy, healthy and fulfilled lives, and Jesus's prime role was showing people how to live in a way that cared for and welcomed everyone. When he spoke to me, he articulated a version of Catholicism that is about reducing marginalisation and oppression. It's about how you treat refugees, people in prison, homeless people – people who are pushed aside by society. 'Our relationship with God is served far more by that than by observing laws,' he said.

Fr McVerry drew parallels with Jesus Christ's conflict between religious leaders at his time, who also believed that serving God was primarily about obeying laws. 'Jesus came along and very clearly said, "What God is interested in, is compassion,"' Fr McVerry said.

Fr McVerry himself is very compassionate towards people in the Church whom he disagrees with. But he also has some refreshing views and takes on the Church. He told me he feels the Church would only ordain women as a last resort – when it's run out of men – and if women priests only happen that way then he's not in favour of it. He doesn't seem too gone on clericalism anyway, and would prefer the Church was run in a more democratic and less hierarchical way. He explained to me that the Church seems to not focus on social justice as much as it should. 'Church leaders are generally elderly men who have grown up with the understanding of a God of the law. So the whole concept of social justice being at the heart of the Bible is new to them,' he said.

Priests and bishops have told Fr McVerry that they 'know nothing about refugees' or they 'know nothing about housing' so they think they can't come out and speak strongly about it. He obviously does not agree. 'I think the Church is called to be prophetic. Prophets don't have to have the answers – prophets just point out the injustice, and they leave it to the experts to find the answers,' he said.

Fr McVerry talks in a way that makes the values of the Gospel feel more relevant to today. For example, he spoke about how we need to scale our personal or material sacrifices against the sacrifice that Jesus was able to make – which was his life. 'We live in a culture which has elevated individualism over the common good, and the Gospel is the exact opposite. And so when you get people who object to social housing in their community, because the value of their house might go down, I find it very hard to reconcile that with the following of Jesus,' Fr McVerry said. 'Jesus was a radical.'

He put his half-full paper cup of tea down on the floor, and Tiny finished it. Fr McVerry explained that I'm not supposed to read the Gospels and interpret how they relate to me individually and how I should live: it's supposed to be about how we live as a community. So the Bible is more like a manifesto than a book of rules.

He told me that he wants to change the Church 'from the inside'. He said the wealth and power of the Church, two things it was never supposed to have, compromised it. Becoming powerful makes you incapable of understanding the lives of the most marginalised and the poorest. 'The worst thing happened to the Catholic Church in Ireland because it got such a powerful position,' he said.

Fr McVerry explained that pockets of the Church are doing great work on housing and homelessness, but the institutional Church as a whole is not as strongly engaged in the kind of activism required to force change. 'The Church should be shouting from the outside,' he said, but at the moment that kind of activism is seen as 'more peripheral than central to the Church's mission'.

Direct provision, housing and climate change are major social issues that will be occupying front pages and Dáil debates for years to come. They feel to me like the most natural key social causes for the Irish Catholic Church. Taking a stronger position on both would have the added benefit of helping to invest in and protect the future of the faith.

This is not just about the greater social good, though that obviously should be a major motivation. This is about bringing people back. And there's no point telling the flock things they already know and expecting the lost sheep to hear it.

I know that the Irish Catholic bishops have a strong view on the injustice of the homelessness crisis, and I know that the Church is in favour of stopping climate change, and I know that there is, sporadically, excellent work being done by the clergy to help people in direct provision.

But the point is, not a lot of people know that. If I was back where I was two years ago, I would have made no effort to seek out the views or positions of the Irish Catholic Church on the social issues I care about. And how likely would it be that I would ever hear the contents of a pastoral letter?

The Church is not going to willingly and quickly reform some of its more controversial views, which makes it hard for some younger people to go back. Why can't the Church make it a little bit easier for us in a way that would not compromise any of its views?

I have reasonable expectations for the Irish Catholic Church. I know, for example, that I may genuinely not live to see a Catholic Church that relaxes or reforms its opposition to LGBT+ people. But I think it would be fair and reasonable to expect to see a Church that can move to the forefront of the biggest social issues that we face as a society in the not-too-distant future.

Some people would criticise the Church for trying to involve itself more in these movements, particularly those on the left who have been doing most of the work on direct provision and climate change. For some people, the Church will never be able to make amends or atone for what it's done. To be honest, there are some people who would be suspicious if the Irish Catholic Church found a cure for cancer. I understand – I've been there myself. But I think, among those people who would be most critical or cynical about the Church getting involved in more social justice movements, there is probably a cohort who wouldn't mind if the Church collapsed in on itself and we saw parishes vanish. I do mind, and so do lots of other people.

If the Church does nothing, if it remains sitting on the sidelines bemoaning all the lost morals of an Irish society that includes reproductive healthcare and marriage equality, it will fail. And it will be its own fault for failing. The Irish Catholic Church needs to weigh up if it believes it will be worth having a future Irish society that has almost totally lost the religion completely just so it can say it loudly opposed abortion at every single opportunity. Even for those who believe that abortion is wrong and a sign of Irish society failing, are those people sure that is the only Catholic cause that matters at the moment?

One of the key missions of the institutional Irish Catholic Church is advocating for the faith, which to me means reaching out to people and trying to bring them back to the Church. I don't feel particularly welcome at the moment, based on the public utterances of some of our most senior clerics. It appears the Church is sitting with its hands folded, waiting for young people to realise they've been wrong all along and come crawling back in atonement.

The Church actually has lots of values in common with young Irish people who advocated for major social change over the last few years. Both are interested in social justice, both believe the planet needs to be protected, both believe in resolving homelessness and welcoming refugees.

I know from talking to my friends that I can't be the only one who feels this way about the Church. I have no doubt that some of those my age who advocated for major social change could feel the same way as well. If they wanted to, it is not beyond the realms of possibility for at least some of those young people to come back to the Church – just like I did – but it's not going to happen on its own. The Church needs to be willing to put the work in to make sure people can hear what it has to say about issues in Irish society that go beyond sexuality.

Chapter 16

It's summer, and I'm 21. I have spent months travelling alone, waking up in a different hostel in a different city each week. Tragically, I only ever went as far as Yorkshire, Aberdeen or Bristol.

I was studying journalism in Cardiff at the time. I was desperate to get into the industry and I had spent that entire summer in a neurotic frenzy trying to get as many internships or work-experience placements at newspapers as I possibly could. Most were unpaid, of course, and depended on me appealing to college friends to let me stay with them or borrowing money from my parents. I do regret this, now that I understand how much damage it does to put a barrier between people who can't afford to work for free and a profession like journalism. But please don't underestimate how little I knew about anything when I was 21.

It was 2012 and the British press was in ribbons. The year before, the true scale of the phone-hacking scandal had been laid bare by a newspaper investigation. A State inquiry had followed, as had the closure of the *News of the World*. Even without such a colossal scandal, the UK print industry was already struggling to make money.

The future looked bleak. A smarter person would have seen the signs and selected a more secure career. And eight years later, I have already seen two vicious redundancy processes at two separate media companies myself. But I loved journalism to the point of obsession and refused to let go. My grand plan was to try to get placements in England, Ireland, Scotland and Wales to maximise my chances of getting a job after I graduated by having experience in different countries that I could easily move to if required. I managed to emotionally harass enough editors to set up enough placements across the UK and Ireland to pretty much fill my summer.

Following the closure of the paper, former *News of the World* reporters started appearing in the newsrooms of local papers where I was doing internships. A Scottish journalist who had worked at the *News of the World* had just been hired at a paper I did a placement with in Aberdeen. He used to scream things like 'IS ANYONE GOIN TAE ANSWER THE FUCKEN FONE?' Once, an ambulance roared past with its sirens blaring, and when nobody in the newsroom reacted he almost went into cardiac arrest. He showed me his old *News of the World* press card and would delight in telling me horror stories from his time at the paper.

I worked at a newsroom in Bristol that was built on top of an in-house printing press, sadly no longer in use. The older hacks told me they used to know their deadline was close when the room started to shake, because it was a sign they'd turned on the printer and were starting to put the paper to bed. That same newsroom had a bar in it, also sadly no longer in use. I did a placement at *Private Eye* where I had to file everything physically on paper for Ian Hislop. He did not have a computer in his office, and would edit your copy with a red pen before handing it back to you to fix. I loved it there because whenever you rang someone and told them where you were calling from, they would instantly say, 'Oh no.' *Private Eye* posted the legal letters they received all over the walls as a badge of honour, and one day I found a dead pigeon in a bin.

That summer, a wave of redundancies was rolling across UK newsrooms and I would often collide with it. I arrived in Leeds to do a placement with the *Yorkshire Evening Post* right when lifelong staff were suddenly being made redundant as the paper's parent company scrambled to cut costs. The newsroom was absolutely massive. It was a symbol of another time, when a big regional paper needed a newsroom as big as a whale's belly. Under the tables were big boxes of cuttings from the older reporters who still sat down with scissors and Pritt Stick to cut out and collect all of their work. I'm not sure I know anyone who still does this now.

My first week was spent watching furious, devastated reporters empty their desks into cardboard boxes. I was embarrassed because I felt like my presence was aggravating.

I was scrambling to get into an industry that these people were being forced out of. A very kind reporter called Juliette did her best to try to keep my placement running as normally as possible, even while her colleagues were losing their jobs all around her. She was such a nice person that I wondered if maybe this had turned into a flaw, and was how she got landed with shepherding clueless cub reporters like me from one end of our placements to the next.

Juliette handed me what should have been a pretty easy assignment. An older man had been repeatedly contacting the newspaper about a flood in the basement of his council house, which the council was refusing to resolve. Terrified of the innumerable ways I could fuck up this very basic task, I carefully read and reread the letter he had sent in as many times as I could before finally picking up the phone and calling him.

This old man had quite the tale to tell. This was not just another newspaper story: it was about a widowed man who felt abandoned. It was about how he had been ignored and dismissed by the council or disingenuously placated with a series of false promises. It was about how angry he was and how lonely he was. It was also, in fairness, a story about a flood in his house.

I'd say I spent a good hour on the phone to this man, becoming increasingly more emotionally invested in his sorry tale. I asked him about his late wife, his interest in sports and how much he loved reading the paper. (As you can see, the news desk was not keeping me particularly busy.)

I was feeling very sentimental about the fact that this man had turned to the newspaper for help. That's a phenomenon that still makes me feel a little awestruck. You wouldn't believe the things that people tell you when they call up a newspaper in desperation. Maybe Fr Bourke's suggestion that all priests should be trained counsellors should apply to journalists as well. But then again, there are some things that people tell you that you could never prepare for.

I had totally lost sight of what my assignment was: to collect the facts and arrange them into a story in time for that day's deadline. Instead, I had grown obsessed with becoming some sort of intermediary between this man and the council and bringing his problem to a resolution.

So devoted was I to my little quest that I even ignored his raging sexism. He had a theory that the council press office was taking advantage of my gender and the fact I would clearly not understand what plumbing was.

The council press office was absolutely baffled by the zeal with which I was approaching this story, as though it was one of the greater injustices of our time. Eventually, Juliette noticed me slamming down the phone to the press office in frustration – *All the President's Men*-style – and came over to investigate how I was getting on.

She stared at me, po-faced, as I talked her through the many twists and turns of my impromptu crusade for justice.

'OK,' Juliette said, with the patience of a saint. 'Let's see your notes.'

I handed them over to her. She quickly picked out a couple of straightforward, accepted facts and one or two relevant quotes. Strengthening her case for imminent beatification, Juliette even sat down and helped me write a very standard, very easy 400-word story: the facts, the man's quotes and the council's response. That's all I needed to do.

The next day, when the older man called back, she offered to take the call and explain that this was unfortunately as much help as the *Yorkshire Evening Post* could offer at this time.

'I know this is the centre of your universe right now, and it feels like the most important thing in the world,' she told the man on the phone, 'but we can't always find space to do all of the stories that matter to everyone.'

I watched her as she hung up, feeling very sheepish. 'Don't worry,' Juliette said. 'Before you know it, you'll be just as jaded as the rest of us.'

Dejected, I dearly hoped she was right. Maybe one day I'd be a hardened hack, navigating the world with a healthy scepticism and a really cool takes-no-shit attitude. As I come to the end of my first decade in journalism, I'm sorry to say that has never happened for me. If anything, I've gotten worse.

———— ✿ ————

I've always been a bit of a sap for human interest stories. I have cried at my desk in work more than a few times over the years. There are parts of interviews with people that, even at this relatively early stage of my career, I know I will never forget. There was a woman who was trying to steer herself through the grief of a fatal foetal abnormality diagnosis, knowing that she had to wait for her dying baby to pass away naturally in an Ireland where a termination for medical reasons was illegal. There was a man who, while still grieving for his wife, had taken up a campaign to reform the transparency around the deaths of women like his partner in Irish maternity hospitals. There have been a few times when I've put down the phone and had to quickly leave the newsroom to disguise the tears. Once my boyfriend joked that he worried he was going through life operating on only 20 per cent of his emotional capacity because he could see by comparison I was clearly on 120 per cent.

People assume that journalists are so overexposed to the bad things of the world that we become emotionally immune to the human tragedy that goes with them. My experience is different. Something usually needs to be an exceptional occurrence to make it onto the front page of a newspaper. I like that every day a newspaper comes out it feels like it's tacitly endorsing the theory that badness in humans is exceptional. It's one of the reasons I wanted to come back to work in Ireland so badly. This country never seems to grow indifferent to personal tragedy. We get to know the victims of car crashes and murders from a respectful distance. I think Irish people tend to go towards empathy rather than invasion. 'Imagine,' people whisper, rustling the pages of the newspaper as they read with interest. 'Isn't it desperate?'

The best part of the job, by a country mile, is getting to talk and listen to so many people. On the campaign trail, I've watched people gently eviscerate a taoiseach's policies with their hand on his arm and a pained expression on their face. 'I know you're trying your best, but ...' I spoke to a man who now has a framed copy of the Irish constitution on his wall because he was so proud that he was picked to be part of a citizens' assembly on constitutional reform. When a tale of personal tragedy is published in the paper, strangers will often get in touch the next day asking if there is anything they can do to help. If I only get to be a journalist for three more years or thirty more, I know one thing now for a fact: people are so good.

When I was a naive student journalist, I was obsessed with the hidden and unhidden malevolence in the world. I saw things in a very black and white way. I was dangerously devoted to finding the bad in people who were in power. I seemed to think there were institutions and governments and agencies that operated only to make the world a worse place. Many of those organisations have a problem with self-preservation that helped to add fuel to my questionable world view. But the longer I spent writing about the bad things that people or governments do, the more I started to realise that a lot of bad is never intentional. Some is, for sure, but often the negative things that states do can be the result of genuine human error or misunderstanding.

Even before writing about someone who was clearly and unambiguously doing something bad, I would get a little pang in my stomach thinking about them opening up their email looking for a right of reply. I worried about them worrying about the story in the paper. I know, right? Journalists are supposed to be tenacious and dogged. I just felt bad for some of them.

Journalism turned me into a little softie and an eternal optimist about the world. This cheery view of mine became even more extreme in early 2020, when the global pandemic hit.

When we realised Covid-19 had arrived on the island of Ireland, in the unassuming bodies of people walking off planes, our little corner of the world seemed to change overnight. Sitting on the couch on a Friday evening, watching the Taoiseach's address to the nation, I had the strange sense that I had stepped outside my own body and was watching this all happen from very far away. The addresses from the government were so strange and scary they seemed almost cinematic, as though they had stolen the dialogue directly from an apocalyptic thriller. Our whole lives were upended. It was like a *Truman Show* moment, as though someone had tripped and the cardboard set of our world had fallen apart.

I could say that the viciousness of the virus made us confront mortality, but it was more accurate to say it let mortality confront us. It crept out of news reports where I read about people who had died and saw ages like 28 or 31. I practised deep breaths in and out while I read, imagining not being able to do that on my own. The virus took people we love, with no regard for their vitality, and reduced them to their vulnerabilities. There's such a darkness to that phrase 'pre-existing conditions'. The age limits the government imposed on who should 'cocoon', though well-meaning and protective, felt a little arbitrary and unfair. But age really wasn't 'just' a number anymore: it was a level of threat. The everyday became existential. One morning my boyfriend took a breath from his inhaler in front of me – something I must have seen him do hundreds of times before. It chilled me. I left the room, consumed with worries I couldn't say out loud.

Sleep was elusive. I lay awake and thought of the people close to me who were most at risk, and worried about this unseen threat seeping into the family home like a noxious gas. Is it in their house already? I was incensed with anger when I heard about idiot visitors who kept showing up. There was a sense of helplessness about not being able to control the lethal carelessness of other people. When you fall in love, you realise your happiness is in someone else's hands. In this pandemic, it's like the lives of our loved ones are in the hands of strangers.

We worked from home and sometimes, by the time we had eased into the evening, life could almost pass for normal.

Then our phones would beep simultaneously. A news alert. The day's death toll.

When I went to the shop to buy my paper, I was shocked by how thin it was – how thin all of them were. Advertising was decimated, and sports writers were suddenly idle. Supplements about arts and entertainment were no longer required. But the number of people reading articles online rocketed upwards; subscriptions increased. Everyone wanted to understand what was happening.

I was assigned a little job by the paper at the start, which I adored. Stories I'd spent a long time on, finding out things that would have made headlines in another life, weren't appropriate anymore. So I was asked instead to focus on seeking out the good in the crisis and write about the people doing what they could to help.

Restaurateurs who had lost almost everything overnight started making meals for nurses and doctors and delivering food to older people imprisoned at home by fear. People who had lost their jobs rallied together to volunteer to help those who were isolated and most at risk, and took heartbreaking care to do so from a safe distance. This was all in the first few days. The immediate and overwhelming instinct from people was to help each other. I was often blinking away tears when writing up those stories. It was a tonic.

People started writing in to the paper, making promises to themselves and each other about the things that they would do first when this was over. The roaring majority of them were promises to hug their loved ones when they could finally see them again. When I read them, they made me emotional. My job was to write back to some and arrange for them to give us more information or photographs so that they could go into the paper. I struck up conversations over email with a few of them. All of their messages were filled with good wishes for me and my family. After a few days, I felt like it'd turned into a task that kept me buoyed through the chaos of the pandemic.

I ended up having a long conversation with one woman who sent in a beautiful promise about going to see her son and his partner in America when it ended. She's a front-line worker, working with people who have intellectual disabilities. She ended up telling me that she's a survivor of domestic abuse, who finally found the strength to leave her partner with the support of her son. She sent me a picture of him and his partner, and I told her they were a very handsome couple. 'Yes they really are handsome, even if I do say so myself, but they are far more lovely people than handsome could ever express. They really are,' she wrote back. 'I certainly do have a story, but doesn't everyone really? It's just that some are not lucky enough to survive to tell the tale.'

I felt more conscious of the struggles of other people, and it started to make me more generous with my patience for others. The individualism that dominated our lives before was destroyed shockingly quickly. It would have made sense if, at a time when everyone was so afraid, we all turned in on ourselves. But instead, everyone was looking out for each other. The tropes from the politicians were right: we seemed closer together when we had to stay further apart.

During the pandemic I felt like the goodness in the world had been amplified. I felt totally raw with emotion most of the time. I was also hypersensitive to the beauty of things that meant absolutely nothing to me before.

I was cooking one day when I heard loud birdsong on my chaotic city-centre street for the first time in five years. I dropped a saucepan as if it'd burnt me, dropped everything I was doing and wandered over to the window to listen, in a daze. Was this new? Or was this always there, I just couldn't hear it before? Everyone in the city talked about the birdsong. There were a few times when I turned off the radio in confusion, convinced the sound of the birds was too loud to be coming from outside. Humanity has devastated the natural world; it makes sense to me that disasters for humanity are opportunities for nature. Foxes were spotted scooting across abandoned streets in the heart of the city. When I went outside to each my lunch in the hot, silent summer days, birds seemed braver. They came right up to me for little scraps.

Songs floored me. I was walking by Grand Canal one morning, listening to the radio, when 'Let's Go Fly a Kite' from *Mary Poppins* came on. It was like an emotional ambush. I was sitting on the couch one day when 'Somewhere over the Rainbow' came on and I felt smothered with upset. I was seeing fewer people, but I was talking to more people. We all swapped notes about our new, tense existences. 'Have you been crying?' 'Have you been able to sleep?' 'Are you OK?'

I was reading the newspaper on a Saturday morning, and I saw a picture of a mother and son hugging. Brackets in the picture caption explained that the mother and son lived together, as though it was excusing them for touching each other after this emotional reunion. I had to abandon the newspaper completely. A minister went on social media and made himself available to take questions from the public. He was bombarded, and most of the first swathe of queries were the same: 'When can we hug each other again?' I had to put down my phone when I read that too.

I said at the start of this book that I felt like life was in lower definition when I wasn't indulging in my faith. Letting myself see God in lots of things allowed life to be brighter and better defined. In the midst of the pandemic, I felt like the definition of everything had been turned up so high that it was blinding. Life was like an overexposed photograph.

I also said before how I thought Catholicism was sociology for optimists. We want to believe that everyone is fundamentally good. This is hard sometimes. People can hurt us on a small scale, and we see the awful inequalities and injustices in the world on a large scale. But when the world was going through one of its worst moments, it was easier than ever to believe that most people are good. My faith in humanity was replenished to its absolute maximum.

So those first few weeks of lockdown were very spiritual for me. When I had the most faith in the world, I also had the most faith in God. Now, that doesn't mean that I believe that God is present when people are good and absent when people are bad. Once it was stripped back to its bare minimum, our existence felt more poignant than before. During the pandemic it was impossible for me to believe that there was not a God. I understand that the human toll of Covid-19 could make other people feel the exact opposite: that there could not be a benevolent God who would allow a world where such a vicious and devastating force could exist. I couldn't see God in the virus, but I could see God in the humanity of our response to it. Simple existence on earth felt more meaningful in those weeks. It made me feel certain that there is something else there for us.

There was bad stuff as well, of course. People were terse and short with each other in supermarket aisles and on footpaths in the park. We started to lose our patience with each other and sometimes passed judgement on the actions or priorities of others. Some of us also found a zeal for policing our neighbours, and for a while Ireland started to hark back to its pious curtain-twitching past. (I wondered if any of those Catholic 'restorationists' took any joy in that.) But these bad things tended to come over time, when the lockdown went on for longer and our collective patience started to fray. Good was our first instinct. Our immediate reflex was to try to help other people.

I heard loud music on our street on a locked-down Saturday night and I was startled by how strange it sounded. The soundscape of our street had always been late-night karaoke and a potpourri of different shouting accents from hens and stags. We lost all of that overnight at the start of the lockdown. I went to the window in my room to see where the music was coming from – was it an illicit house party? Maybe it was an audacious lock-in? When I looked outside I could see the allure of the music had drawn all the neighbours from the apartments I could see across the street to their windows, too. All these young adults with their hands pressed against the glass, all at home at midnight on a Saturday. Normal human desires like wanting to go out for a bop suddenly seemed very romantic.

I started to count my blessings. I looked at my boyfriend, the person I was lucky enough to be sharing a lockdown with, and marvelled at all the beautiful little coincidences that had to happen for me to end up with such a wonderful person. I steeled myself before I answered the phone to my mother, and breathed a sigh of relief when I found out everything was OK at home. I was thankful that I still had a job, but I started to appreciate that my career was not everything. Like everyone, I found this time hard. But I know that it would have been significantly harder for me had I not had the comfort of being able to pray.

I was allowed to leave the house sometimes to interview people for work, and I was on high alert for hearses. I started to feel like I was seeing them everywhere. The tragic image wasn't just the coffin on the inside, but that the hearse was often being driving on its own. Death was making its presence felt at precisely the moment when we couldn't mourn properly.

I've been to lots of non-religious weddings, but I've never been to a funeral that wasn't Catholic. I suppose that's a sign of our gradual growth out of the faith. When we lose the older Irish generation, so many of whom are kindred in their belief, I wonder if the lifelong devotion to Catholicism, which so many Irish people had, will die with them too.

During the pandemic everybody was mournful for the loss of the Irish art of mourning. Families don't bury their dead in Ireland: communities do. Denying people that during the pandemic felt especially cruel. I cried while I watched a viral video of a small rural village in Kerry adapting for a funeral they can't attend. People paid their respects by standing, metres between them, all along the tiny village street and rural country roads that the family would drive along to get to the church.

In the generic day-to-day, the impending certainty of death isn't something people like to talk about. Sometimes, I feel like Irish people use the occasion of death to get it all out in one go. We wear death for days, and we lay it out for everyone to see. I remember being picked up under my arms as a small child and lifted up so that I could peer inside an open coffin where an elderly relative lay. I was unfazed.

Dead bodies felt normal. Dead bodies are normal. For me, death is inextricable from Catholicism. I don't know how I would even mourn without religion. The painful loss of life is always swaddled in the comfort of knowing that it isn't the end. I've been to so many funerals where people have talked sincerely over little triangle sandwiches about a butterfly that had flown into the church during the ceremony or a bird that was perched on the newly engraved headstone as the coffin was lowered into the ground. Anecdotal evidence would find ways to meaningfully connect the deceased to these little creatures. Everyone would agree that this was a fleeting visit from the lost loved one, and everyone would be very matter-of-fact about it. It's a sign of the afterlife, and people cling to that sort of poignancy because it helps. Your mortal grief feels like it's being dwarfed by the mystique of what happens to people after they die, and that can feel nice. It's a reminder that we're the ones who are just passing through.

One thing that Catholicism has always gotten right has been letting people indulge in their grief when others die. Ireland, in particular, has thrived in the field of mourning, all the way back to the keening women, who would join together to wail in grief. Knowing that we will see the deceased again is never used as an excuse to force people to be stoic. It's a precious thing to be able to believe that death is not the end. Even if the worst happened and I found out we were wrong about God, I'd still be grateful that people of faith had had that. I have vowed to make sure I always keep that belief, no matter what might happen in future to my relationship with the Church. I think it would be too much to lose that too.

Mortality, and all of the discomfort that comes with it, reared its head at the start of the pandemic and never went away. Everything suddenly felt very frail to me. After three months of not seeing them, government guidance finally let me sit outside one sunny day with two of my best friends at a strange distance. They were the same two I had been sitting with when I made my drunken confession about thinking I might be Catholic. Sitting chatting in our little triangle, I had a comforting thought. 'We've all stayed alive,' I thought, marvelling at our thirty respective years of vitality. 'Isn't that great?'

I've never thought about my death in any great depth before, but Covid-19 made me stand nose to nose with it. To be honest, this felt like a spiritual blessing. I had always had a clear idea of what a life well lived would mean to me, and it was based on success, memorability and impact. I don't want to get too pious about it, but the years when I was most vehemently chasing those things were the years when I was most opposed to religion. It's nice to remember your smallness in the world sometimes. Thinking about my life in that way made it seem silly for me to prioritise personal success over nicer goals, like just being a good person and trying to live a good life. I still wanted to make myself matter, but in much simpler ways. I just wanted to be good.

People talk about how everyone prays in the end, but I think that's a truism from a pre-pandemic world. Covid-19 was a great big reset socially, politically and economically, but spiritually as well. Everyone got to have the Scrooge experience: a sudden shock that lets you see your life in a very different way. I am sure people had just as intense spiritual experiences as me during the pandemic, without feeling the desire to go back to an organised religion like Catholicism.

I just know that during the pandemic, the evidence of this good in people made my desire to be Catholic stronger because I already believed in God. The difference in opinion comes down to a question of faith. I know now that I need religion, but I appreciate that others don't. I think that society is better when those of us who want to can have faith. Religion doesn't have a monopoly on good people, and society is capable of being good when it's secular. I believe Catholicism can improve society in the same way I feel certain types of politics can improve society – it's a strong belief but not one which I consider I should be able to force on others. I just knew that I had made the right decision. I'd known for a long time that I wanted to go back to the Church but would flitter and worry about it. Now, I was bolstered by absolute certainty that it was the right thing to do.

The pandemic was still roaming through Ireland precisely two years after I first started to think differently about Catholicism. I sat down one day and used an advanced search to go back and look at the things I was saying on social media in the days leading up to the referendum on the Eighth Amendment.

Posts on social media are not an accurate reflection of a whole person – particularly when they're written and posted during a very intense time. A lot of people were arguing with each other on the internet that week. But some of the things that I said sound very hard and cold, and are undoubtedly not things that I would say now. I read, with disappointment, old rows I had with people. I read bitter remarks that I made as soon as someone criticised me or something I had written. I seemed very abrasive and defensive, and convinced that anyone who was criticising or disagreeing with me was trying to personally attack me.

In the two years since then, some of my views have changed. The core ones have not. I still think, as I did then, that the Church's position on women and LGBT+ people is morally wrong. I still think there were Catholic conscientious reasons for voting Yes in the referendum on the Eighth Amendment, and of course in the marriage equality referendum.

But I now understand some things that I did not before. I realised quickly at the start of this process that appetite for Church reform is probably much stronger within the faithful than it is among former outsiders like me. In many ways, this reminds me of repeal. We heard for such a long time how the status quo was the most popular option and that trying to change things would be too difficult or chaotic. I think, in both instances, a quieter majority was not best served by the much louder interests of a more powerful minority. Just because we can't hear what some of the laity or clergy are saying about the things that are wrong with the Church doesn't mean we should assume we know what they think.

I think I understand better now how the things that put me off Catholicism – the outrageous quotes from bishops, the seemingly cold and institutional responses to the latest scandals – were more likely to be the product of a cultural row than a spiritual one. These arguments that we see in the media are never about God: they're often more about perception and politics. Homophobia and archaic attitudes to women's health are part of the Church's teaching but I don't believe they can be permanent parts. At the start of 2020, Bishop Cullinan wrote a pastoral letter to mark the New Year. In it, he spoke about how a new 'culture' in Ireland was basically unravelling Christianity. He blamed this culture for undoing the rights of the unborn and made a veiled reference to its promotion of marriage equality for same-sex couples as well.

'We must wake up to what is happening and, with the grace of God, change the culture from within,' he said.

The bishop said that 'about 90 per cent of our people are not coming to Church regularly so we must go out and seek the "lost".' He challenged parishioners directly, asking them if they were happy with the way society is going. He called on them to play their own role, in a kind of vocation of sorts. He said the Church needed 'a vision of a Church which, starting from a relationship with Jesus, looks outward rather than inward'.

I think what Bishop Cullinan wants to do to Irish social culture is exactly the inverse of what I would like to do to the Irish Catholic Church's culture. When I think of the words 'culture' and 'Catholic' together, I think of a culture of secrecy, a culture of shame and a culture of sanctimony. I also think of a culture of cronyism.

I think that, for a long time, the way the Church has been run and the way it has portrayed itself has been done in a way that suits those who are at the top of the institution. I don't claim to speak for anyone but myself, and I know there will be devoted parishioners who would be horrified if the Church changed, for example, its position on LGBT+ people. But I do know that the blame for the rapid decline of the Church, and the possibility of it having no real future in Ireland, lies more with the institution than it does with any changed 'culture' in Ireland.

Bishop Cullinan's idea, for the faithful people of the Catholic Church to try to change Ireland for the better, isn't a radical one. In fact, it sounds exactly like the *raison d'être* for modern Irish Catholicism to me. But I think for that idea to have any real prospect of success in Ireland this century, the Church needs first to allow itself to be changed from within for the better. Don't you think it's telling how clerics like Bishop Cullinan talk about the Catholic Church and Irish society as though they are two distinctly different things?

People like me believed that they were for far too long. I acted as though the Church was the last haven for those who held the kinds of prejudices we were busy trying to eliminate from Irish society. That kind of thinking is driving people away from the Church, and it carries the horrifying collateral of driving people away from God as well.

People like me have a right and responsibility to try to change those aspects of the Church from within, if enough of us feel strongly enough that it should be changed. And senior clerics have a right to respond to that criticism and concern, but a responsibility to listen to it as well. Too often, the hierarchy of the Irish Catholic Church appears to do the former without ever considering the need to do the latter.

It's probably easier and more comfortable for the people in charge of the Church to blame the 'culture' for the decline of the faith. It's a much more romantic idea to imagine bishops standing with pride and grace as this great, unstoppable tide of Irish social degeneracy sweeps around them. Unfortunately for them, that's not what's happening now at all.

While I appreciate the limits of my 30 brief years of experience on this earth, it appears to me that Ireland's culture, while still diverse and more inclusive of all faiths and none, happens to fit with Christian ideals now more than it ever did before. We don't need to go over old ground again, but it's disappointing that we got to this point in spite of the Catholic Church rather than with it.

You cannot raise people with Catholic values, teach them about Catholic beliefs and give them everything they need to be guided by their own conscience only to turn around and tell them they're wrong when what they're saying doesn't suit you.

I think that kind of arrogant ethos is often the germination of what eventually turns into these 'culture wars', where we have the Church and its spokespeople on one side of the debate and the rest of us on the other, locked in a bitter dispute. Sometimes these disputes end in the improvement of Irish society, but it never results in the Church improving.

Without reforming itself, I'm worried that any attempt by the Catholic Church to help improve and direct society will be regarded with suspicion and possibly even revulsion by a lot of people. If the Irish Catholic Church doesn't change itself, it will lose the ability to change anything else. The sins on this island are not a finite list of consensual same-sex marriages and difficult individual decisions to terminate a pregnancy. With all due respect to the sincerity with which people in the clergy oppose the recent legal changes, the Church needs to get over recent social reforms and realise that it has a greater contribution to make – which it is throwing away over a fixation on abortion and marriage equality. I don't believe the Church should ever change its position on the right to life of the unborn. I do believe it needs to change the attitude with which it approaches such a sensitive issue, and separate itself from the anti-abortion extremists of the world who are carrying out emotional terrorism on women in the name of God. As for the issues of same sex marriage and ordaining women: I think it's a question of when, rather than if, these things will change.

I don't want to start or lead some kind of movement. I don't want to be a protagonist in the story of how the Church changed. I've only just managed to figure out that I want and maybe need to go back. I think that if I find people within the Church who have similar beliefs to me, then maybe we can find some space to discuss how to move this forward. I am right at the start of this process myself, and I understand that people who are smarter and more articulate than me have already been trying to do this for a long time. Organisations like We Are Church have already been organising around reform of the Church in Ireland. All I'm trying to do here is have my voice heard, and find out how many other people might feel the same.

I would rather be inside the Church and watching it try to change than outside and bitching about why it isn't bothering to. I am trying to be as respectful as possible when I say this, but frankly the scale of what is at risk is too great to trust senior bishops to do the right thing.

I mentioned before how my primary school teacher taught me about the importance of unconditional faith. It is very different to blindly unquestioning faith. A priest told me, what feels like a long time ago now, that your faith doesn't have any strength at all if you don't challenge it. I feel like I've put mine through the wringer. But I have it now.

I have chosen this. I've made an active decision about my faith and made it something that I want to have rather than something I was simply born with.

Catholic priests often try to temper the occasion of a wedding day by gently reminding the couple that this is just the first day of a hopefully long and happy relationship. I feel the same now about religion. Deciding to go back is probably, in the grand scheme of things, the easier part. Faith requires work and nurturing, and it will challenge me and probably at times seem like it's deserted me. I feel as strong and positive and ready for that as I think I possibly could.

The first part is showing up, deciding to be present. I'm here. I exist. I'm a Catholic.

Acknowledgements

Thank you to Deirdre Nolan at Gill for having the patience and the skill to take our long, deep chats about faith over coffee and help me to turn them into a book. I wouldn't have had a clue how to do this without you, and you've made a strong case for your own sainthood. Thank you to copyeditor Emma Dunne and to everyone at Gill who worked so hard to help bring this together, especially Aoibheann Molumby, Ellen Monnelly and Teresa Daly.

I want to thank Jennifer Bray, my comrade in the world's smallest book-club. You encouraged me to write this, so it's my turn to return the favour. I hope I get to see your debut in a bookshop soon.

Thank you to all my family and friends for the support. I'd like to mention everyone at the Ard Scoil, particularly all of 'the lads' who made my time there such a joy. When I was fourteen I vowed I'd thank Bean de Paor when my first book came out, because she was such a fantastic champion for writing when I was lucky enough to have her as an English teacher. I'm so delighted that she was part of this book and I'm really grateful for her help.

I want to say a special 'thank you' to the people of the Irish Catholic Church who met my questions and queries and anxieties with such warmth and kindness. It's a testament to how much compassion and friendship I was shown that I can't possibly list everybody, but you all know who you are. I will be grateful for the rest of my life to the clergy and laity who helped me through this.

I want to save the last and largest 'thank you' for the two people without whom this book would not have existed. Thank you to my mam for doing her best to raise us to understand how important faith is. I wasn't grateful for it at the time, but I am now.

And to Peter O'Dwyer. I am so lucky to have you. Thank you, I love you.